BIRDWATCHING BY TRAIN

Where to go in Britain

Alison M O Harris & Nigel G Harris

RSPB
The Lodge
SANDY
Beds
SG19 2DL
LIBRARY

BIRDWATCHING BY TRAIN

Where to go in Britain

Alison M O & Nigel G Harris

Transport Publishing Company

Published by Transport Publishing Company
128 Pikes Lane
Glossop
Derbyshire
SK13 8EH

British Library Cataloguing in Publication Data

Birdwatching by Train
1. Ornithology
2. Railways
I Harris, A M O II Harris, N G

Printed in Great Britain for
Transport Publishing Company
128 Pikes Lane
Glossop
Derbyshire
SK13 8EH

ISBN 0 86317 179 6

Cover pictures: *Barn Owl (Courtesy Sefton Photo Library); (clockwise from top left)
Ardlui, Forsinard,
Shoreham-by-Sea and Hayle Estuary.*

Contents

BIRDWATCHING SITES COVERED

1	Adur Estuary	26	Jumbles Reservoir
2	Arlington Reservoir	27	Kennet Valley
3	Arthog Bog	28	Kinghorn
4	Attenborough	29	Leighton Moss
5	Baron's Haugh	30	Loch Lomond
6	Berney Marshes	31	Lochwinnoch
7	Bookham Common	32	Longcross
8	Breckland	33	Montrose Basin
9	Central Wales	34	New Forest
10	Chichester Harbour	35	Peak District (North)
11	Clowes Wood	36	Peak District (South)
12	Conwy Valley	37	Penarth Flats
13	Craigellachie	38	Radipole Lake
14	Delamere Forest	39	Rye House Marsh
15	Dent	40	St Bees Head
16	Epping Forest	41	Sandwell Valley
17	Exe Estuary	42	Sandy
18	Filey Brigg	43	Severn Estuary
19	Firth of Clyde	44	Shibdon Pond
20	Formby	45	South Norwood Country Park
21	Forsinard	46	The Swale
22	Frodsham	47	Tamar Estuary
23	Hampstead Heath	48	Tyne Estuary
24	Hayle Estuary	49	Tywi Estuary
25	Hillbre Island	50	Wrabness

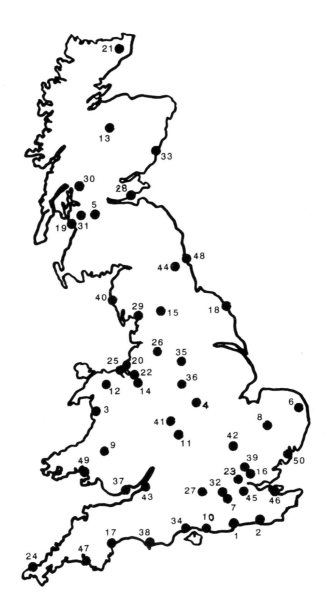

Introduction

Purpose of this booklet

The aim of this booklet is to provide details of access by rail to good birdwatching sites in Britain. It does not concentrate on birdwatching from trains, although this can be very profitable in some areas of the country. Without any steering to attend to, and without prejudicing safety, one's whole undivided attention can be paid to passing birds. Moreover, birds tend to get used to passing trains and are generally not too intimidated by them. For instance, when researching for this booklet, we had a very long and close look at a female kestrel which was flying along, parallel to the train, whilst we were travelling along BR's Arun Valley line between Horsham and Arundel, in Sussex. Indeed, birds of prey are well seen by train, and we can recommend the Doncaster - York line for kestrels, and the Yeovil and Barnstaple - Exeter lines for buzzards.

This book is not really about the birds you can see on railway stations, either. However, mention should be made of some highlights e.g. the Lesser Black-Backed Gulls which seem to inhabit Cardiff Central's parcels platforms. In some rural areas, considerable birdlife may exist within the station buildings. At one station we know of in rural Lincolnshire, swallows nest in the waiting room on one platform, whilst the fence on the other platform is a favourite perch for a Spotted Flycatcher.

The real focus of this booklet, however, is on good birdwatching sites close to stations. We have taken 'close' to mean within 1500 metres (therefore within easy walking distance), but many are much closer and, in some cases, access to nature reserves is even direct from station platforms. With the increasing concern over the environment, many people (especially those with interests in wildlife and the countryside) are paying special attention to their own lifestyle. This may be to see if they can play their part in avoiding forecast environmental disaster, or possibly just the traffic congestion that is becoming endemic in, and en route to, the countryside. One of the biggest problems, however, is the lack of information relating to "environmentally-friendly" activities, including access to the countryside. This booklet attempts to fill part of that information vacuum.

Sites Chosen

The 50 sites set out in this booklet have been chosen carefully. We have already seen that all lie close to railway stations, but we have generally only included stations with good rail services. We have also attempted to include a selection of habitats, as well as a spread of sites around the country (see map on page 7), so that some are available to every reader as day-out possibilities, as well as others being particularly suitable when on holiday. However, these 50 sites are by no means the only ones, and readers are encouraged to find their own favourites; the North York Moors, Malverns and North shore of the Thames estuary are all easy to explore, for instance. Fitter readers will also find that walking between stations gives access to a whole new set of birdwatching opportunities.

Format of the Main Text

We have adopted a standard format for the main text, with a two-page spread being used for all sites. An icon gives a general impression of whereabouts the site is in Britain, whilst a map shows the local rail network; these maps are, however, not to scale, and not all stations are shown. Information as to the rail services at the selected station generally applies to the standard off-peak services (usually operated between the peaks on Mondays to Fridays, and on Saturdays). We have also given an indication of services at other times, both in the peaks, and on Sundays (where applicable). If there is no Sunday information, then the service is similar to that on a weekday, but less frequent; note also that a Sunday service is generally applicable on Bank Holidays. It is generally advisable to check detailed train timings before setting out, either in the Great Britain timetable (for which timetable numbers are shown here), or by phone to the nearest BR information office (see your local telephone directory for details).

Information on rail services is followed by details of the sites chosen. Habitat and likely birds to be seen are set out, as well as the distance to the start of good birdwatching country, and directions from the station. Some indication of the extent of local facilities is also included, should the reader need shops, a drink or an overnight stay. In some cases, mention is also made of other nearby sites worth investigating .

How to Maximise Your Chances

Although we have chosen what we believe are some of Britain's best and most rail-accessible birdwatching sites, there are inevitably a number of other factors which come into play. We cannot guarantee that you will see thousands of birds at every location every time, but we set out here some basic ground-rules which will enable you to maximise your chances.

Sites where there are a range of habitats obviously tend to do better than those where one type of vegetation predominates. Moreover, water is as important for birds as it is for humans, so it usually pays to visit pools, ponds and rivers.

Secondly, birds have their own routines, determined by time of day and the weather. Some birds are nocturnal, and visits on a Summer evening are likely to be most profitable. Many birds are busy both early and late in the day, which (unfortunately) means that midday visits may find everything quiet; birds also tend to rest and/or shelter in wet and windy weather.

Thirdly, some of Britain's birds are only around at certain times of year and, even those which are resident here tend to be most active in particular months—early Summer is usually a good time, for adults birds are then finding food for their young. Indeed, early Summer is also a good time of year to catch our Summer migrants arriving, but remember that early Summer may be April in Cornwall, but July in the North of Scotland. Conversely, other species only come to Britain in the Winter, and trips to see Brent Geese in the Hampshire estuaries will be wasted at other times of year.

Fourthly, your behaviour will also determine what you see. If a party of ten of you go singing through a wood, all dressed in bright red anoraks, then birds will disappear pretty quickly. However, with patience, most birds can be approached reasonably closely if you remain quiet and avoid sudden movements. Your behaviour also has an effect in the long-term.

Following the birdwatchers' code of conduct (see below) means that the environment stands the best chance of supporting many birds, and that landowners are less likely to take objection to your presence.

Birdwatchers' Code of Conduct:

1. Birds come first.
2. Protect habitats.
3. Keep away from nests.
4. Keep dogs on a lead, or leave them at home.
5. Don't drop litter.
6. Be careful not to start fires.
7. Don't advertise information relating to rare birds.
8. Respect the rights of landowners—get permission if required.
9. Keep to footpaths and shut gates.
10. Keep quiet – you'll disturb birds less, and will see more of them.

Fifthly, you should be prepared for the conditions. Walking boots, sufficient layers of clothing for the conditions, waterproofs, food (and additional chocolate if it is cold), a map and compass, and a note at home of where you expect to be, and when, will all minimise the possibility of anything going wrong. Remember that the weather in Britain can be very changeable, and better be prepared than sorry.

Lastly, there is unfortunately an element of pure chance when birdwatching. In particular, woodland birdwatching can be very variable, since small birds tend to roam around woodland areas; a short walk will increase your chances of coinciding with singing warblers or a flock of tits. However, by keeping your ears and eyes open, by looking behind you from time to time (as well as in front), you can make conditions favourable. A companion is invaluable for that second opinion of the rare bird you thought you saw fleetingly through the trees, for keeping a better lookout, and for helping you out should you get into problems (e.g. getting lost) .

Other Relevant Books

A number of other books set out good birdwatching sites, although they invariably concentrate on access by car. However, they may provide more detailed information on some of the sites mentioned here. Moreover, good birdwatching walks may be had between stations, and the following publications contain useful information for the fitter reader on sites not included here because of their distance from rail stations:

Gooders, J. (1989)   "The New Where to Watch Birds" (224pp. A5 size, Papermac, London; £4.99)

Parslow, J. (ed.) (1983) "Birdwatcher's Britain" (256pp. A5 size, Pan Books Ltd., London/ Ordnance Survey, Southampton; £6.99).

RSPB (1989)   "Where to go Birdwatching: a Guide to RSPB Nature Reserves" (128pp. 20cm*20cm, BBC, London; £6.50).

Scott, B. (1987)   "An Atlas of British Bird Life" (208pp. A4 size, Country Life Books, Twickenham, London; £15.00).

In addition to such books, a large number of field guides are now available to help birdwatchers identify the birds they see when out, but space precludes a listing of these here. However, we do recommend the use of Ordnance Survey maps, and so the 1:50000 Landranger series map number, as well as the National Grid reference, has been quoted for all the main sites.

Birdwatching Organisations

The main birdwatching organisations in Britain are the Royal Society for the Protection of Birds (RSPB), with over 800,000 members, and the much smaller but research-orientated British Trust for Ornithology (BTO). Their addresses are:
RSPB, The Lodge, Sandy, Bedfordshire. SG19 2DL.
BTO, The Nunnery, Nunnery Place, Thetford, Norfolk. IP24 2PU.
In addition, many county naturalists' and wildlife trusts maintain reserves good for birdwatching.

British Rail Services and Fares

British Rail (BR) provides a wide range of passenger rail services throughout Britain, from InterCity expresses racing the length of the country (and soon to France and Belgium too) to commuter services in South East England, and local and regional services elsewhere in the country. As the organisation is so large, they have subdivided it into three businesses, broadly as described above; these are InterCity, Network South-East and Regional Railways. Despite this subdivision, however, many aspects of the service are similar. Information about all three is available from local travel centres or from the twice-annual national timetable. And, importantly, the fare structure is also generally similar.

Railway fares in Britain are fairly complex, but a range of fares are available to suit leisure travel for purposes such as birdwatching. If you do insist on travelling at peak times in and around London, or on crack InterCity business trains, then rail travel can be expensive as well as busy; ordinary single and return tickets are available for this purpose. However, at off-peak times (between the usual journey to work peaks during the week, and at evenings, weekends and Bank Holidays), rail travel can be surprisingly cheap.

For local journeys, day returns are available at little more than the single fare. Restrictions often limit their use on weekdays to after 09:30, but at other times there are usually no restrictions at all. They cover returns for distances of up to 50 miles (slightly further in South East England). Over this distance, the equivalent ticket type is the Saver, which is also valid for return travel on any day up to a month later. If you can avoid travelling on Fridays, Summer Saturdays, and certain other days (usually around Bank Holidays), an even lower fare is available—the SuperSaver.

The above ticket types are probably those most suitable for day trips, or other trips from home, but Railrovers are also available if you intend to travel a great deal (perhaps within a small area whilst on holiday). For instance, a Rail Rover is available for the whole of

Scotland, both for one week and for two. Two types of Rail Rovers are generally available—those where travel has to be on consecutive days, and those FlexiRovers where travel can be purchased for a number of days within a period e.g. three days within seven.

Fares (whether for single or return tickets or for Rail Rovers) can be even cheaper if you have a railcard. Pre-purchase of an annual card at a price of between £10 and £20 can enable Young Persons (under 26), Senior Citizens (over 60) and Disabled Persons to travel at a discount of 34%, whilst there is also a Family Railcard for family groups travelling together on single or return journeys.

For longer distance travel, seat reservations can be made, which will ensure that you get a seat on your desired train. Seat reservations generally cost £1, but this covers any number of trains for the same journey, and up to four passengers booking (and travelling) together. However, fees for seat reservations are often waived around Bank Holidays.

You may be interested in taking your cycle with you, which is generally feasible except on those parts of the rail network which are underground (e.g. BR's Moorgate - Finsbury Park line in London, as well as all those parts of London Underground which are below the surface). At a cost of £3 per journey, cycles may be taken in the guards' van or luggage compartment, but pre-booking is essential, since some trains are restricted and others offer very limited space. Full details are given in a leaflet called "The Rail Travellers' Guide to Biking by Train", available from most major stations, where other general queries (including those about RailRovers and Railcards) may also be answered.

Services and Fares on Other Rail Systems

Services on London Underground and the Tyne and Wear Metro are generally slower than on British Rail, because they stop at all stations. However, they are generally much more frequent, and most services run at intervals of 15 minutes or less; in Central London, headways can be as low as every two minutes. Services also operate consistently right through the day, between 0600 and 2400, on most routes.

In both cases, although single and return fares are available, better value is had by travelcards, permitting unlimited travel across all or part of the relevant systems. Such travelcards are also available for some of the other metropolitan areas (e.g. West Yorkshire), but may only be valid after 09:30 and at weekends. Different travelcards are available, depending upon which parts of the local network ('zones') are required; many also offer travel on the local bus network too.

Acknowledgements

The production of this booklet has only been possible with the help of a number of people. John Senior and his staff at TPC have been instrumental in the physical production of the booklet, and have supplied many useful suggestions as to its contents and format. British Rail have provided considerable facilities for us in travel and advice, and particular thanks must go to our main contact, Mark Livock of Regional Railways.

Two of our birdwatching friends have contributed information about parts of the country they know well. Mark Harwood has provided useful data for a number of sites in North West

England, whilst the same task has been carried out by Bill Heslop for North East England. By spreading the research workload, the book has come to fruition much more quickly and, as they are experts in their own areas, more accurately too. However, any errors remaining are our responsibility, but we cannot be held liable for inaccurate information, or not seeing the birds indicated.

Wishing all readers easy and successful birdwatching by train,

Nigel G Harris
Alison M O Harris
Crystal Palace
LONDON SE19.
January 1992.

Guillemots are strictly marine birds coming ashore only to breed and during storms. Breeding occurs in colonies on cliffs in the North and West, such as at St Bees (see page 96).

ADUR ESTUARY

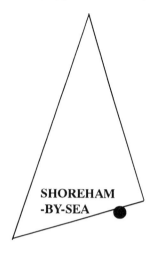

SHOREHAM
-BY-SEA

County:	West Sussex.
Map:	Sheet 198 ref. TQ216048.
Nearest Station:	Shoreham-by-Sea.
Distance (m):	400.
Timetable no.:	186.
Rail Service:	20 minute frequency local service from Brighton

alternately to West Worthing, Littlehampton via Worthing and Portsmouth Harbour via Worthing, Chichester and Havant. Hourly fast service between London Victoria (via East Croydon and Haywards Heath) and Littlehampton/ Southampton. Southampton portion also calls at Chichester, Havant and Fareham.

Time taken: Brighton 14 mins, Littlehampton 30 mins, Chichester 37 mins, Portsmouth 80 mins, Southampton 92 mins.

Peaks: some additional commuter services to London Bridge.

Connections available at Brighton for Eastbourne and Hastings; at East Croydon for Sydenham, London Bridge and Thameslink to King's Cross, Luton and Bedford; at Ford for Arundel, Horsham and Littlehampton; at Barnham for Bognor Regis; at Havant for Petersfield and Guildford,

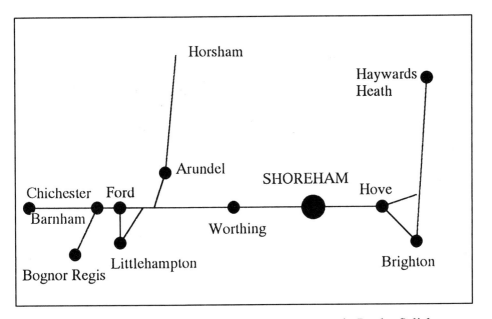

and at Southampton for Bournemouth, Poole, Salisbury and Winchester.

Local Facilities:	The town centre provides a full range of shops, cafes and pubs befitting a sizeable town.
Habitat:	Estuarine mudflats and (to the North West) some saltmarsh.
Access:	Turning left (South) outside the station, the town centre lies between the station and public footbridge spanning the harbour, from where good views can be obtained (binoculars required at low tide).
Likely Sightings:	Waders, gulls, terns, cormorant; linnet etc.
Best Time of Year:	Spring and Autumn migratory periods, when more interesting waders may appear.
Nearby Sites:	Much of the South Coast's estuaries are easily accessible from the Havant-Chichester railway line—see section on Chichester Harbour. Chichester's gravel pits 2km South-East of the city have also provided interesting ducks and waders in the past.
Notes:	

ARLINGTON RESERVOIR

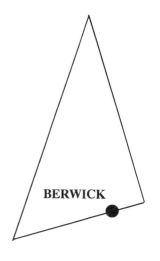

BERWICK

County:	East Sussex.
Map:	Sheet 199 ref. TQ530075.
Nearest Station:	Berwick (Sussex).
Distance (m):	800.
Timetable no.:	189.
Rail Service:	Hourly local service from Brighton via Lewes to Eastbourne. *Time taken*: Lewes 11 mins, Eastbourne 15 mins, Brighton 26 mins. *Peaks*: Services extended from Eastbourne to Hastings. *Connections* available at Lewes for Newhaven, Seaford, Haywards Heath, East Croydon and London Victoria; at Eastbourne for Hastings; at Brighton for Worthing, Shoreham-by-Sea and Chichester.
Local Facilities:	The village has a shop and a public house. Outside tables are set out by the reservoir.
Habitat:	Reservoir with surrounding farmland and young woodland.
Access:	A public right of way runs around the reservoir from the road due North of the station.
Likely Sightings:	Ducks, grebes, terns, waders; crows; warblers and finches.
Best Time of Year:	Reasonable all year round, with terns and warblers in Summer, and ducks and finches in Winter.

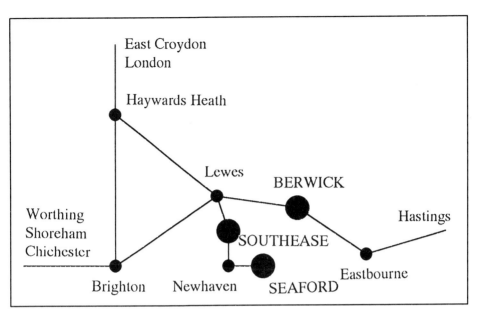

East Croydon
London

Haywards Heath

Lewes

BERWICK

Worthing
Shoreham
Chichester

Hastings

SOUTHEASE

Brighton   Newhaven   SEAFORD

Eastbourne

Nearby Sites: Southease station on the Seaford branch is on the South
Downs Way with ready access to downland with its smaller
species including yellowhammer, blackcap, whitethroat
and nightingale. Seaford itself offers seawatching from the
Eastern end of the promenade, by the foot of the cliffs.

Notes:

*The Mute Swan is a huge waterbird, being 150cm when fully-grown. Favouring fresh water, it is the commonest of Britain's
swans, and may be distinguished by an orange bill (grey-blue in juvenile birds), rather than the yellow of the Bewick's and
Whooper swans. [N.G. Harris*

ARTHOG BOG

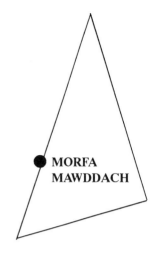

MORFA
MAWDDACH

County:	Gwynedd.
Map:	Sheet 124 ref. SH635145.
Nearest Station:	Morfa Mawddach.
Distance (m):	50.
Timetable no.:	76.
Rail Service:	Seven trains per day each way along the picturesque Cambrian Coast line between Pwllheli (via Harlech and Barmouth) and Machynlleth (via Tywyn). Some trains extended beyond Machynlleth to Shrewsbury or Aberystwyth. The station is a request stop. *Time taken*: Barmouth 6 mins, Harlech 28 mins, Machynlleth 49 mins. *Connections* available at Machynlleth for Aberystwyth, Shrewsbury and Wolverhampton, and at Minffordd for the privately-owned steam-operated Ffestiniog Railway.
Local Facilities:	Public conveniences only. However, 3km to the North, and reached across Barmouth bridge (a toll footbridge), lies the resort of Barmouth.
Habitat:	Very varied: woodland, rough grazing, mudflats, saltmarsh.
Access:	Immediate access can be gained from the station to the Penmaenpool-Morfa Mawddach railway walk, which runs through woods to the East. A pleasant walk of 4km can be

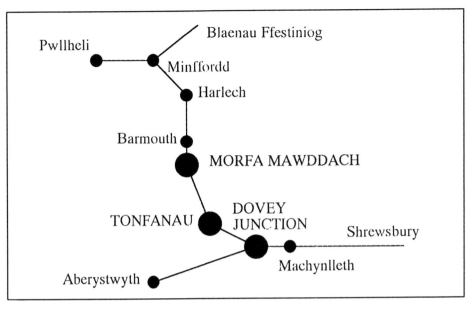

had by following this to SH638145 before bearing Northwards across a marsh (footpath reasonable) to reach the estuary near a stand of coniferous trees. Return to the station can be around the small wooded hill of Fegla Fawr, skirting a small area of mudflat.

Likely Sightings: Woodland species (tits, warblers, nuthatch, treecreeper etc. and pied flycatcher in Summer); crows and wagtails on the marsh; gulls and waders in the estuary; possibility of red kite.

Best Time of Year: Late Spring, when Summer migrants are newly-arrived.

Nearby Sites: The muddy lagoon of Broad Water is only 1.5km from Tonfanau, four stops South of Morfa Mawddach. Some trains stop at Dovey Junction station, where the lines from Aberystwyth and Barmouth converge, West of Machynlleth; this station is in the middle of a reedbed, and time spent waiting for a train can be profitably used.

Notes:

ATTENBOROUGH

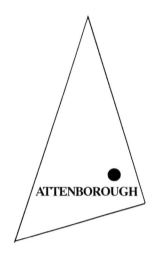

ATTENBOROUGH

County:	Nottinghamshire.
Map:	Sheet 129 ref. SK522342.
Nearest Station:	Attenborough.
Distance (m):	500.
Timetable nos.:	56, 80 .
Rail Service:	Hourly service from Crewe (via Stoke-on-Trent and Derby) to Nottingham.

Time taken: Nottingham 9 mins, Derby 20 mins, Stoke 70 mins, Crewe 100 mins.

Connections available at Nottingham for Grantham, Peterborough, Chesterfield, Sheffield, Newark and Lincoln; at Derby for Matlock, Burton and Birmingham; at Stoke for Stafford, Macclesfield, Stockport and Manchester; and at Crewe for Liverpool and Chester.

Local Facilities:	Very few.
Access:	Turn left (South) outside the station; access is off to the right when the road turns sharply left.
Habitat:	Lakes (disused gravel workings) and reedbeds interspersed with small stands of trees and overgrown hedges.
Likely Sightings:	An extremely wide range (over 200 species seen), including tits, warblers and tree sparrow; ducks, geese, grebes, waders (e.g. snipe, ringed plover), heron;

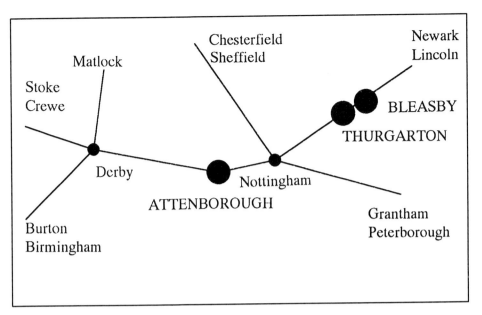

kingfisher; common tern.

Best Time of Year: Late Spring, when Summer migrants are newly-arrived.

Nearby Sites: Other gravel workings in the Trent valley easily accessible by rail include those between Thurgarton and Bleasby on the Nottingham - Newark line (two-hourly service six days per week, 20 mins from Nottingham; one km from either station).

Notes:

BARON'S HAUGH

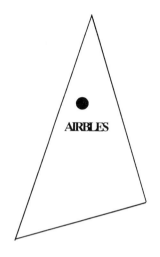

AIRBLES

County:	Strathclyde.
Map:	Sheet 64 ref. NS750555.
Nearest Station:	Airbles.
Distance (m):	1000.
Timetable no.:	226.
Rail Service:	Half-hourly service from Dalmuir via Glasgow Central, Newton and Hamilton to Motherwell (alternate services extended to Coatbridge Central) .
	Time taken: Motherwell 2 mins, Hamilton 5 mins, Coatbridge 11 mins, Newton 15 mins, Glasgow Central 32 mins, Dalmuir 56 mins.
	Connections available at Motherwell for Edinburgh, Carlisle and Lanark; at Newton for Mount Florida and Pollokshields; at Glasgow Central for Barrhead, Kilmarnock, Ayr, Paisley and Greenock; at Dalmuir for Dumbarton.
Local Facilities:	Shop/Post Office on the main road near the station.
Habitat:	Woods, scrub, meadow, lake, marsh, river bank.
Access:	Entering from North Lodge Road, the main entrance is through coniferous woodland, with paths leading through meadows and scrub to the three RSPB hides. Continuing Westwards, the riverbank can be followed until a set of

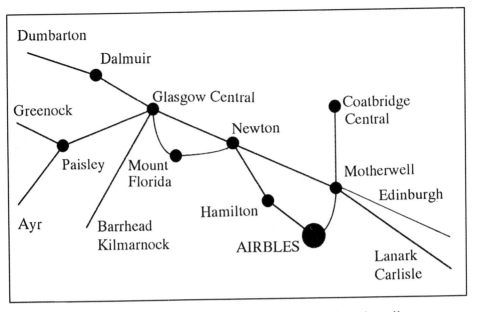

steps leads up to the right shortly before the railway
viaduct; these come out under the electricity pylons over
Harvest Drive. This is a cul-de-sac off Clyde Valley
Avenue, itself off North Lodge Road, thereby completing a
circular walk of about 3km.

Likely Sightings: Waders, gulls, ducks, swans, cormorant; kestrel, crows; tits,
warblers; kingfisher.

Best Time of Year: Winter (for ducks) or early Summer (to include all the
migrants).

Notes:

BERNEY MARSHES

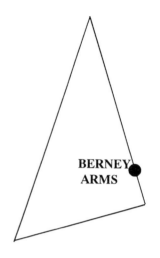

BERNEY
ARMS

County: Norfolk.
Map: Sheet 134 ref. TG460054.
Nearest Station: Berney Arms.
Distance (m):   0 (Marshland visible from platform).
Timetable no.:   16.
Rail Service: Two trains per day each way between Norwich (via
                   Reedham) and Great Yarmouth. Trains are in mid-morning
                   and mid-afternoon; the station is a request stop.
                   Time taken: Reedham 7 mins, Yarmouth 9 mins, Norwich
                   27 mins.
                   Sundays: At present, all Norwich - Yarmouth trains are
                   being routed via Berney Arms on Sundays, and three are
                   booked to stop on request.
                   Connections available at Reedham for Lowestoft, and at
                   Norwich for Sheringham, Thetford, Cambridge,
                   Peterborough and Ipswich.
Local Facilities: One km from the station is a riverside pub. Otherwise, the
                   only buildings are two farms and a preserved windmill.
Habitat: Saltmarsh, with a scrape.
Access: There is no car access to this isolated (if not desolate)
                   reserve, but it is possible to reach the reserve either on foot
                   or by boat. A walk around the area should include a visit to

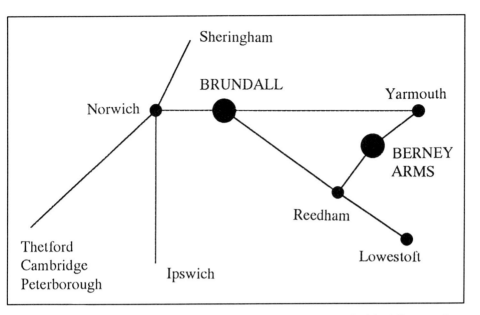

Sheringham

BRUNDALL

Yarmouth

Norwich

BERNEY
ARMS

Reedham

Thetford
Cambridge
Peterborough

Ipswich

Lowestoft

                   the scrape constructed by the RSPB behind (i.e. on the landward side of) the pub; a grassy track leads from the station.

Likely Sightings: Waders, gulls, heron; wagtails, linnet etc.

Best Time of Year: Late Spring, when the marshes are still relatively wet but when the early migrants have arrived.

Nearby Sites: The RSPB's Strumpshaw Fen reserve lies 2km East of Brundall, and provides good woodland and marsh birdwatching alongside the River Yare.

Notes:

BOOKHAM COMMON

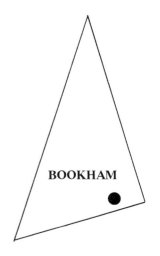

BOOKHAM

County:	Surrey.
Map:	Sheet 187 ref. TQ1 27560.
Nearest Station:	Bookham.
Distance (m):	0 (station footbridge gives limited views of woods; access off platform) .
Timetable no.:	52.
Rail Service:	Half-hourly 'Thameslink' service between Guildford and Luton via Leatherhead, Epsom, Sutton, West Croydon, Crystal Palace, Elephant, Blackfriars, King's Cross and St Albans.
	Time taken: Guildford 15 mins, West Croydon 25 mins, King's Cross 66 mins, Luton 107 mins.
	Peaks and Sundays between Effingham Junction and London Waterloo via Leatherhead, Epsom, Wimbledon and Clapham Junction.
	Connections available at Guildford for Portsmouth, Aldershot, Reading and Woking; at Leatherhead for Dorking; at Epsom for Wimbledon and Clapham Junction; at Sutton for St Helier; at Norwood Junction for Sydenham and London Bridge; at Blackfriars for LUL's District line, and at King's Cross for LUL and InterCity services.
Local Facilities:	The village centre is not very close to the station, but there

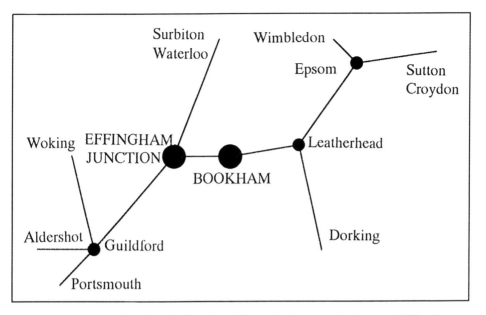

	is a hotel close by. There is also a pub close to Effingham Junction station.
Habitat:	Common land, with woods, glades and ponds. Farmland adjacent.
Access:	Entrance to common is off Leatherhead-bound platform.
Likely Sightings:	Tits, warblers, woodpeckers, finches, jay, treecreeper etc. in the woods. Moorhen, coot etc. in the ponds. Pigeons, doves, crows, pheasant, grey partridge in the adjoining farmland. A 4km walk to Effingham Junction may be beneficial, but a map and compass will be needed, as the common is very easy to get lost in.
Best Time of Year:	Early Summer, when Summer migrants as well as residents will be present. In particular, a wide selection of warblers may be found within the woods.
Notes:	

BRECKLAND

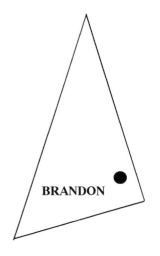

BRANDON

Counties: Norfolk/Suffolk.
Map: Sheet 144 ref. TL785872.
Nearest Stations: Brandon.
Distance (m):   300-1000.
Timetable no.:   18.
Rail Service: Two-hourly service from Norwich via Thetford to
                   Cambridge via Ely.
                   Time taken: Thetford 10 mins, Ely 20 mins, Cambridge 39
                   mins, Norwich 48 mins.
                   Connections available at Ely for King's Lynn and
                   Peterborough; at Cambridge for Royston, Bishop's
                   Stortford and London; and at Norwich for Sheringham,
                   Great Yarmouth and Lowestoft.
Local Facilities: The town has the usual selection of local shops and pubs.
Habitat: Woodland (mostly coniferous), riverside and heath.
Access: Two distinct areas are easily accessed from the station.
                   Open country of fields interspersed with woods can be
                   reached at 785882 (North of the station, passing the
                   sawmill en route) whilst the Little Ouse river can be
                   followed either East or West from a point only 200m South
                   of the station. Westwards leads to heathland, whilst
                   Eastwards gives rise to coniferous forest, and a pleasant

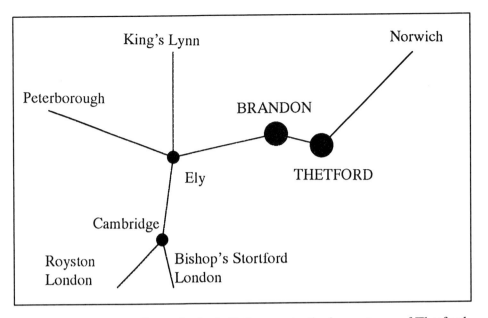

King's Lynn

Norwich

Peterborough

BRANDON

Ely

THETFORD

Cambridge

Royston
London

Bishop's Stortford
London

walk can be had all the way to the larger town of Thetford (12km), with its hourly service of fast Norwich - Birmingham/Liverpool trains.

Likely Sightings: Tits, goldcrest, redpoll, crossbill; redstart; whinchat; warblers; woodlark; nightjar; waders e.g. snipe, curlew; stone curlew.

Best Time of Year: Early Summer.

Notes:

CENTRAL WALES

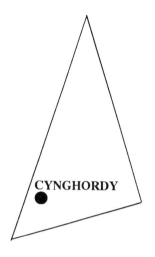

CYNGHORDY

Counties:	Dyfed/Powys.
Map:	Sheet 147 ref. SN802407.
Nearest Stations:	Cynghordy.
Distance (m):	100.
Timetable no.:	129.
Rail Service:	Four trains per day from Swansea via Llanelli and Llandeilo to Shrewsbury via Llandrindod Wells and Craven Arms. Cynghordy is a request stop. *Time taken*: Llandeilo 31 mins, Llandrindod 36 mins, Llanelli 75 mins, Swansea 101 mins, Craven Arms 2 hours, Shrewsbury 2 hours 30 mins. *Sundays*: No Winter service (October-mid May). *Connections* available at Llanelli for Carmarthen and Pembroke, at Swansea for Neath and Cardiff, at Craven Arms for Leominster; and at Shrewsbury for Welshpool, Wrexham, Crewe, Telford and Wolverhampton.
Local Facilities:	None.
Habitat:	Upland rough grazing with wooded valleys.
Access:	Immediate from the station.
Likely Sightings:	Meadow pipit; red grouse; golden plover; dipper, grey wagtail; pied flycatcher, redstart; red kite.
Best Time of Year:	Early Summer.

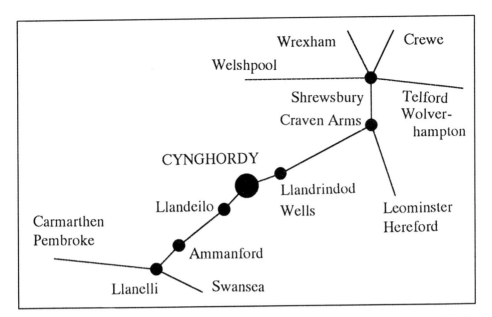

Nearby Sites: Most of the stations along the Central Wales line North of Ammanford also give access to similar countryside. Walks between stations are easily made, and special arrangements are made for Summer Sundays, including the opening of Sugar Loaf Halt, near the summit of the line at Sugar Loaf mountain, one stop North of Cynghordy.

Notes:

CHICHESTER HARBOUR

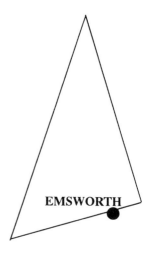

EMSWORTH

County:	West Sussex.
Map:	Sheet 197 ref. SP749055.
Nearest Stations:	Emsworth.
Distance (m):	900.
Timetable no.:	186.
Rail Service:	Hourly slow service from Brighton via Hove, Worthing and Chichester plus hourly semi-fast service from London Victoria via Horsham and Chichester to Portsmouth Harbour via Havant.
	Time taken: Havant 5 mins, Chichester 10-15 mins, Portsmouth 22 mins, Worthing 45 mins, Brighton 70 mins, London 113 mins.
	Connections available at Havant for Southampton, Petersfield and Guildford; at Barnham for Bognor Regis, and at Ford for Littlehampton.
Local Facilities:	Local shops.
Habitat:	Harbour, mudflats, saltmarsh.
Access:	Follow the road South from the station, over the roundabout, and into the marina area. Bear round to the right as the path becomes "Wayfarer's Walk".
Likely Sightings:	Waders (e.g. dunlin, knot, godwits, curlew, redshank); gulls, terns; brent goose; ducks (e.g. wigeon, teal); yellow

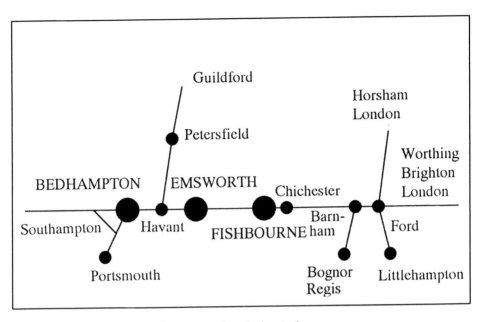

wagtail; sparrowhawk, kestrel.

Best Time of Year: An all-year site, with terns and wagtail in the Summer, passage waders in the Autumn, and brent geese and waders in the Winter.

Nearby Sites: Other stations along the line between Chichester and Portsmouth (e.g. Warblington) also give access to the estuary, but the shortest walk is from Fishbourne (one stop West of Chichester, but served only by the slow services). It is also quite easy to walk along coastal footpaths between stations e.g. Bedhampton to Emsworth; the end of Thorney Channel near Southbourne is a particularly good area.

Notes:

CLOWES WOOD

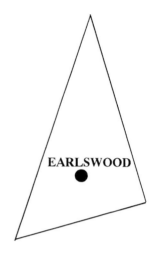

EARLSWOOD

Counties: West Midlands/Warwickshire.
Map: Sheet 139 ref. SP105738.
Nearest Stations: Earlswood, The Lakes.
Distance (m): 100 and 500 respectively.
Timetable no.: 72.
Rail Service: Hourly service between Stratford-upon-Avon and Birmingham Snow Hill via Shirley and Tyseley.
Sundays: No service.
Time taken: Stratford 24 mins, Birmingham Snow Hill 30 mins.
Connections available at Wilmcote (the station before Stratford) for Warwick and Leamington Spa; and at Tyseley for Solihull. Birmingham Snow Hill is only 600m from Birmingham New Street, with its mainline services covering large parts of Britain. There are plans to connect Snow Hill with existing rail services to Stourbridge.
Local Facilities: None.
Habitat: Arable farmland, wood and lake.
Access: Footpaths lead South across the fields off the road 100m East of Earlswood, and North into the woods off the road 500m East of The Lakes.
Likely Sightings: Pheasant, grey partridge; crows; tits, goldcrest,

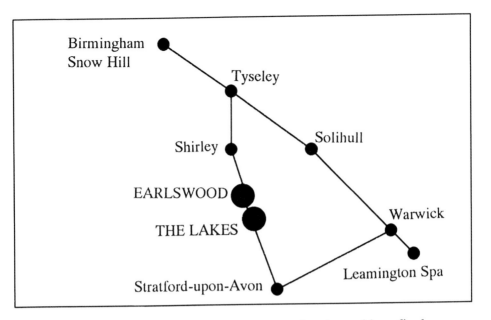

woodpeckers, treecreeper, nuthatch, warblers, finches; ducks.

Best Time of Year: Early Summer, when the warblers as well as the resident species will be present.

Nearby Sites: Other stations towards Stratford give easy access to arable land, with its typical species e.g. yellowhammer.

Notes:

CONWY VALLEY

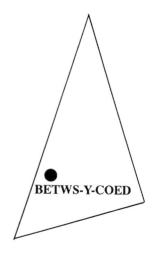

BETWS-Y-COED

County:	Gwynedd.
Map:	Sheet 115 ref. SH792568.
Nearest Station:	Betws-y-Coed.
Distance (m):	200.
Timetable no.:	84.
Rail Service:	Five trains per day between Llandudno Junction and Blaenau Ffestiniog; some service extended beyond Llandudno Junction into Llandudno.
	Time taken: Llandudno Junction and Blaenau Ffestiniog both 28 mins.
	Sundays: Two trains each way mid-May to early September only.
	Connections available at Llandudno Junction for Bangor, Holyhead, Rhyl and Chester, and at Blaenau for the privately-owned Ffestiniog railway to Porthmadog.
Local Facilities:	The village is a known tourist centre, and has local shops, cafes, hotels, a campsite, and the Snowdonia Forest Park information centre, which includes birdwatching material.
Habitat:	Riverside, pine forest, moorland.
Access:	Riverside footpaths from the village near the station; moorland reached through the woods on the Western side of the river.

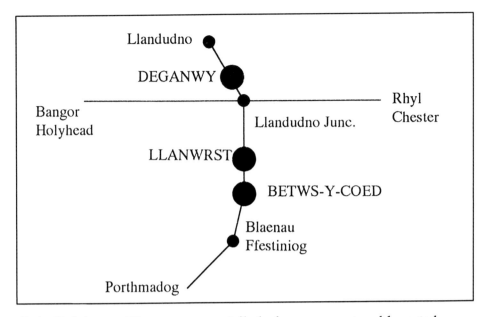

Llandudno

DEGANWY

Bangor
Holyhead

Llandudno Junc.

Rhyl
Chester

LLANWRST

BETWS-Y-COED

Blaenau
Ffestiniog

Porthmadog

Likely Sightings: Dipper, grey wagtail, ducks, cormorant, red-breasted merganser, goosander in the river area; crossbill, siskin, finches, warblers, pied flycatcher, buzzard in the woodlands; grouse, meadow pipit, peregrine on the moors.

Best Time of Year: Avoid the height of the Summer tourist season, when disturbance becomes a problem.

Nearby Sites: Other stations on the Blaenau branch also give easy access to good birdwatching countryside, the best probably being Llanwrst, since it (like Betws-y-Coed) has access to both banks of the river, and to the higher ground to the West. Deganwy station, on the Llandudno branch, has good views of the Conwy estuary, with its waders.

Notes:

CRAIGELLACHIE

AVIEMORE

County:	Highland .
Map:	Sheet 36 ref. NH890120.
Nearest Station:	Aviemore.
Distance (m):	800.
Timetable no.:	231.
Rail Service:	Broadly two-hourly service along the main line between Perth (via Pitlochry) and Inverness. The service runs alternately to/from Glasgow Queen Street and Edinburgh (including two trains which are InterCity services to London, one to King's Cross via Newcastle, the other to Euston via Birmingham). There is also a sleeper service to Euston. *Time taken:* Inverness 45 mins, Pitlochry 63 mins, Perth 95 mins, Glasgow and Edinburgh 2hrs 45 mins each. *Connections* available at Inverness for Elgin, Aberdeen, Dingwall, Kyle of Lochalsh, Wick and Thurso; and at Perth for Dundee and Stirling.
Local Facilities:	The town centre has shops, hotels and guest houses.
Habitat:	Crag, birch woodland and pond. Despite its proximity to the town, the site is remarkably quiet and overlooked.
Access:	Craigellachie National Nature Reserve is reached from a path West off the main street South of the station; the path

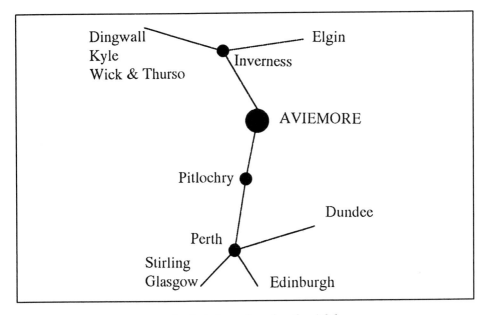

Dingwall
Kyle
Wick & Thurso

Inverness

Elgin

AVIEMORE

Pitlochry

Dundee

Perth

Stirling
Glasgow

Edinburgh

passes the hotels and under the A9 bypass.

Likely Sightings: Peregrine; tits, warblers (especially willow), redstart; waders e.g. common sandpiper; ducks. Possibility of osprey.

Best Time of Year: Early Summer, when the warblers as well as the resident species will be present.

Notes:

DELAMERE FOREST

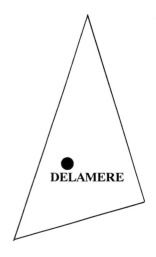

DELAMERE

County:	Cheshire.
Map:	Sheet 117 ref. SJ556704.
Nearest Station:	Delamere.
Distance (m):	100.
Timetable no.:	98.
Rail Service:	Hourly service from Manchester Piccadilly via Stockport, Altrincham and Northwich to Chester.
	Time taken: Northwich 15 mins, Chester 20 mins, Altrincham 45 mins, Stockport 63 mins, Manchester 74 mins.
	Connections available at Chester for Birkenhead, Liverpool, Rhyl, Llandudno, Wrexham, Shrewsbury and Crewe; at Altrincham for Metrolink services to Manchester and Bury; and at Stockport for Bolton, Buxton, Macclesfield and Stoke.
Local Facilities:	Information centre, toilets, shop and pub in the village of Hatchmere, 2km North along B5152.
Habitat:	Woodland.
Access:	Picnic areas and public rights of way lead through the woods from immediately adjacent to the station.
Likely Sightings:	Woodpeckers (all three species); warblers; pied flycatcher; redstart; sparrowhawk; woodcock; grebes in the meres.

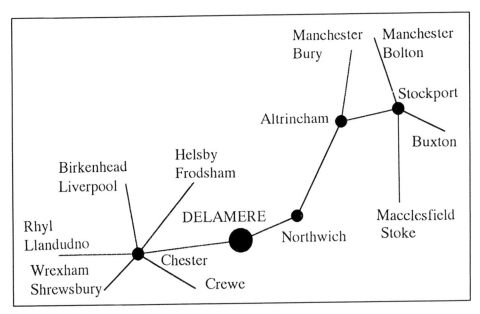

Manchester Bury

Manchester Bolton

Stockport

Altrincham

Buxton

Helsby
Frodsham

Birkenhead
Liverpool

DELAMERE

Macclesfield
Stoke

Rhyl
Llandudno

Northwich

Wrexham
Shrewsbury

Chester

Crewe

Best Time of Year: Early Summer for warblers etc.

Notes:

The meres within the Delamere Forest are home to grebes, including the Great Crested Grebe, a diving bird feeding on fish. [N.G. Harris

DENT

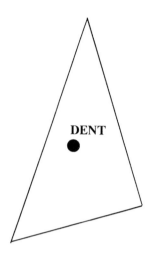

County:	Cumbria/North Yorkshire.
Map:	Sheet 98 ref. SD764875.
Nearest Station:	Dent.
Distance (m):	0 (station is in middle of moorland).
Timetable no.:	36.
Rail Service:	Six trains per day between Carlisle via Appleby to Leeds via Skipton, Keighley and Shipley.

Time taken: Appleby 33 mins, Skipton 42 mins, Keighley 54 mins, Carlisle 75 mins, Leeds 88 mins.

Sundays: No Winter service (October-mid April).

Connections available at Skipton for local services to Leeds and Lancaster; at Shipley for Bradford and Ilkley; at Carlisle for Haltwhistle, Workington, and InterCity services to Glasgow and Edinburgh; and at Leeds for Harrogate, Wakefield, Doncaster, Huddersfield, Selby and York.

Local Facilities:	None.
Access:	Turn right and up the hill outside the station; this road leads to Garsdale after approx. 5km.
Habitat:	Moorland, with some coniferous plantations.
Likely Sightings:	Meadow pipit, twite, wheatear; ring ouzel; curlew, golden plover; red grouse; sparrowhawk, merlin, hen harrier. Unlikely birds seen by the authors include herons and

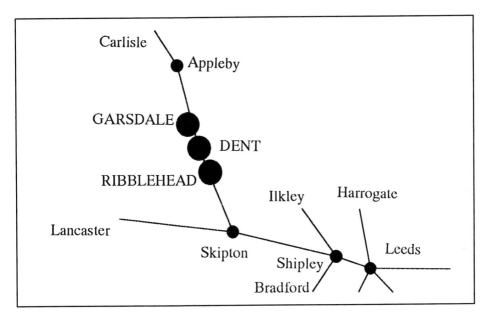

                      escaped parakeets!

Best Time of Year: Summer; Winter conditions can be severe.

Nearby Sites: The adjacent stations of Ribblehead (to the South) and Garsdale (to the North) offer similar birdwatching possibilities.

Notes:

EPPING FOREST

CHINGFORD

County:	London/Essex.
Map:	Sheet 177 ref. TQ400950.
Nearest Station:	Chingford.
Distance (m):	200.
Timetable no.:	20A.
Rail Service:	Twenty-minute frequency service from London Liverpool Street via Hackney Downs and Walthamstow Central. *Time taken:* Walthamstow 11 mins, Hackney 19 mins, Liverpool Street 26 mins. *Connections* available at Walthamstow for LUL's Victoria line (also short walk to Walthamstow Queen's Road for Barking and Harringay); at Hackney for Edmonton and Broxbourne; at Liverpool Street for Ilford, Romford, Southend and LUL services.
Local Facilities:	Public house and parade of shops.
Habitat:	Common land, with woods, glades and ponds.
Access:	Almost opposite the station.
Likely Sightings:	Finches (including Hawfinch), tits, warblers, redstart, woodpeckers, jay, treecreeper in the woods; redwing and fieldfare in Winter. Moorhen, coot etc. in the ponds. Pigeons, doves, crows, pheasant, grey partridge, kestrel on the more open land.

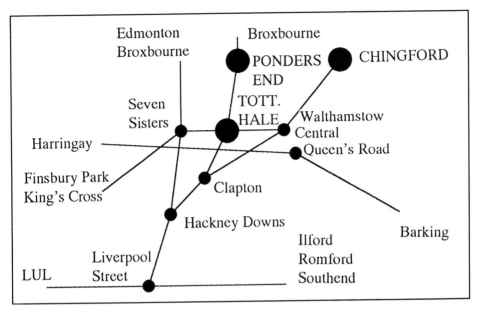

Best Time of Year: Either early Summer (for the warblers) or Winter (for redwing, fieldfare and finches).

Nearby Sites: The lower Lea Valley is surprisingly good for birds, despite its proximity to Central London; easy access is gained to it between Tottenham Hale and Ponders End, including from the stations at Angel Road and Northumberland Park. The river itself holds ducks and kingfisher, whilst linnets and kestrel can be found in the surrounding scrub.

Notes:

EXE ESTUARY

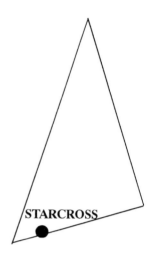

STARCROSS

County:	Devon.
Map:	Sheet 192 ref. SX976819.
Nearest Station:	Starcross.
Distance (m):	0 (views from platform and footbridge).
Timetable no.:	135.
Rail Service:	Broadly hourly service from Exeter Central via Exeter St David's to Paignton via Dawlish, Teignmouth, Newton Abbot and Torquay.

Time taken: Dawlish 5 mins, Exeter St Davids 12 mins, Teignmouth 15 mins, Newton Abbot 23 mins, Paignton 45 mins.

Connections available at Exeter Central for Exmouth; at Exeter St David's for Barnstaple, Taunton, Bristol, Yeovil Junction and Salisbury; at Newton Abbot for Plymouth and Truro.

Local Facilities:	Toilets, local shops and a couple of pubs.
Habitat:	Estuarine mudflats.
Likely Sightings:	Waders (including Avocets in Winter), gulls, terns, Brent Geese (in Winter), cormorant; seaducks such as Red-Breasted Merganser.
Best Time of Year:	Winter.
Nearby Sites:	The Exe estuary is well served by rail, and can also be seen

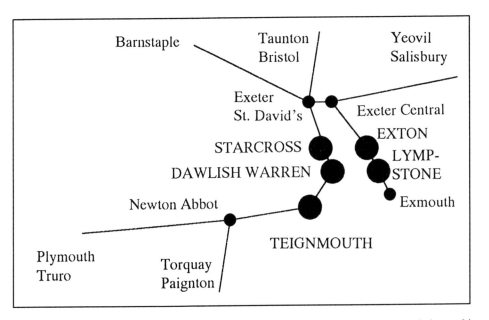

easily from Exton and Lympstone (on the Exmouth branch) and at Dawlish Warren (one stop South of Starcross), where a spit extends out into the estuary. At Teignmouth, the harbour area is also well worth a look for other waders. Note also that ferry services for foot passengers only operate from Starcross (adjacent to the station) to Exmouth, and across the Teign estuary from near the lifeboat house (weekdays only), and these may give good opportunities for birdwatching.

Notes:

FILEY BRIGG

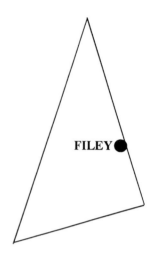

FILEY

County:	North Yorkshire.
Map:	Sheet 101 ref. TA130815.
Nearest Station:	Filey.
Distance (m):	1000.
Timetable no.:	38.
Rail Service:	Nine trains per day (every hour-and-a-half) between Scarborough via Seamer and Hull via Beverley and Bridlington.
	Time taken:: Seamer 9 mins, Scarborough 17 mins, Bridlingt(25 mins, Beverley 53 mins, Hull 66 mins.
	Sundays: No Winter service (October-mid May).
	Connections available at Seamer for Malton, York and Leeds, and at Hull for Goole, Selby and Doncaster.
Local Facilities:	The town centre of this small resort contains a reasonable ran of shops and pubs.
Habitat:	Rocky headland providing vantage point for seawatching; exposed mud at low tide.
Access:	Access to open country is gained most quickly through Chur(Cliff country park, although access to Filey Brigg can also be had by walking along the beach from the town.
Likely Sightings:	Gannet, cormorant, waders, seaducks, gulls, terns; divers, shearwaters, skuas, chats, thrushes and finches on passage.

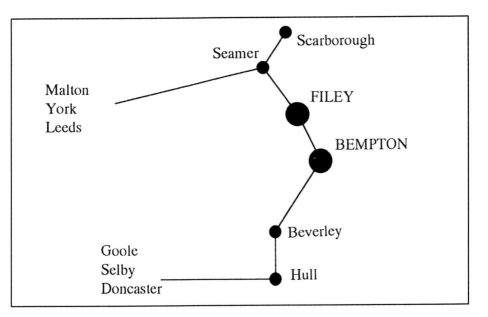

Best Time of Year: During the Autumn migration period, when birds of the open sea may appear close to the shore at such headlands.

Nearby Sites: Bempton's famous chalk cliffs, with their thousands of nesting seabirds, are a 5km walk along a country lane from Bempton station (two stops (15 mins) South of Filey). Gannets, guillemots, razorbills, puffins, fulmars and kittiwakes can all be seen in abundance, especially in early Summer, whilst the RSPB have just opened a visitor centre, shop and tea-shop.

Notes:

FIRTH OF CLYDE

ARDROSSAN
SOUTH BEACH

County:	Strathclyde.
Map:	Sheet 70 ref. NS235415.
Nearest Station:	Ardrossan South Beach.
Distance (m):	200.
Timetable no.:	221.
Rail Service:	Two trains per hour from Glasgow Central via Paisley Gilmour Street and Johnstone, and Kilwinning, one continuing to Largs, the other to Ardrossan Town (also handy for birdwatching).

Time taken: Kilwinning 10mins, Largs 17 mins, Johnstone 31 mins, Paisley 35 mins, Glasgow 45 mins.

Peaks: three services per day continue beyond Ardrossan Town station to Ardrossan Harbour, for connections to Arran.

Connections available at Kilwinning for Ayr; at Paisley for Gourock; at Glasgow Central for suburban services to Motherwell, East Kilbride, Cathcart and Dalmuir.

Local Facilities: The town centre (nearer the Town station) contains a reasonable range of shops, as well as giving access to the harbour, from where boat trips to nearby Horse Island can be arranged - contact RSPB Scottish office on 031-556-5624.

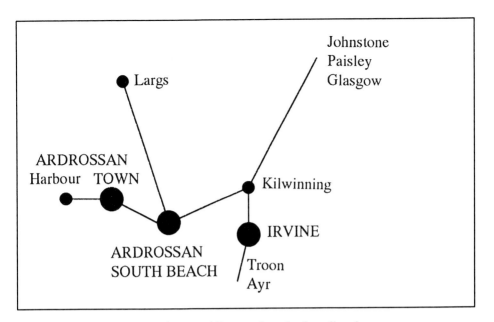

Habitat:	Estuarine mudflats and rocky headlands.
Access:	South of the station, across the main road and green.
Likely Sightings:	Waders (e.g. godwits, plovers, Purple Sandpiper), gulls, terns, cormorant; divers, seaducks such as Eider.
Best Time of Year:	Spring and Autumn migratory periods, when more interesting waders may appear.
Nearby Sites:	The estuaries around Irvine (one stop South of Kilwinning) hold Whooper swans, Wigeon and Golden Plover, whilst South Bay at Troon (two more stops South) is good for waders and the gull roost, which may include some of the rarer species.
Notes:	

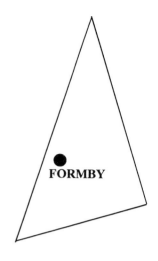

FORMBY HILLS

FORMBY

County:	Merseyside.
Map:	Sheet 108 ref. SD275065.
Nearest Stations:	Freshfield, Formby.
Distance (m):	800(max), 1000 respectively.
Timetable no.:	101.
Rail Service:	15 minute frequency service between Hunt's Cross via Liverpool, Sandhills and Bootle to Southport. *Time taken:* Southport 13 mins, Bootle 17 mins, Sandhills 22 mins, Liverpool 27 mins, Hunt's Cross 42 mins. *Connections* available at Southport for Burscough and Wigan; at Sandhills for Ormskirk and Kirkby; at Liverpool Moorfields/Central for Birkenhead, New Brighton, West Kirby, Chester and Ellesmere Port; and at Hunt's Cross for Warrington and Manchester.
Local Facilities:	Local shops near the stations, particularly Freshfield.
Habitat:	Sand dunes, pine forest, scrub, shoreline.
Access:	Ainsdale National Nature Reserve is reached through the housing estate to the West of the railway.
Likely Sightings:	Warblers, chats, wheatear; gulls; waders e.g. sanderling, knot, dunlin; seaducks such as scoters may be seen offshore.
Best Time of Year:	Avoid popular times in the Summer, when disturbance can

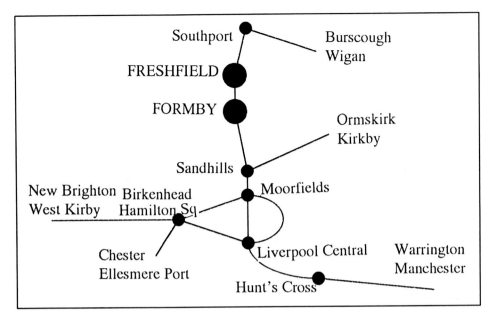

be a problem; Winter is better for the waders.

Notes:

Closely-related members of the same bird families may require either a particularly close look, or will depend upon song for their identification. The Great Tit (above) may be slightly larger and yellower than the Coal Tit (below), which also has a white nape, but the pitch of the voice may be an easier method of distinguishing these two widespread woodland species. [J.H.Hume (2)

The Nuthatch is a woodland tree-climber found mostly in the South of England that may be attracted to bird tables, as here. The Arctic Tern is a Summer visitor to coasts, particularly in the North and West. Good views are required to separate it from its close relative the Common Tern which may, however, also be regularly found at inland sites. Bill colour, and the length of legs and tail are the best distinguishing features. [J.H.Hume (2)

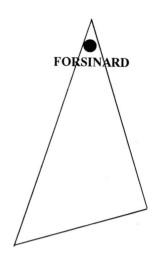

FORSINARD

FORSINARD

County:	Highland.
Map:	Sheet 10 ref. NC892425.
Nearest Station:	Forsinard.
Distance (m):	0 (station is on isolated moor).
Timetable no.:	239.
Rail Service:	Three trains per day from Inverness via Dingwall, Lairg and Brora to Thurso/Wick.
	Time taken: Thurso 45 mins, Brora 48 mins, Wick 49 mins, Lairg 86 mins, Dingwall 2hrs 30 mins, Inverness 2hrs 56 mins.
	Sundays: No Winter service (October-mid May).
	Connections available at Dingwall for Kyle of Lochalsh, and at Inverness for Aberdeen, Aviemore, Perth, Stirling, Glasgow and Edinburgh.
Local Facilities:	The hamlet has a shop/Post Office, as well as a hotel.
Habitat:	Upland moor and bog.
Access:	Views from the road.
Likely Sightings:	Waders (e.g. curlew); crows; linnet, twite; pied wagtail; birds of prey including Golden Eagle, kestrel.
Best Time of Year:	Avoid the Winter, when conditions may be hazardous (the train has had to be dug out of a snowdrift in recent times).
Nearby Sites:	The landscape varies little between Helmsdale and

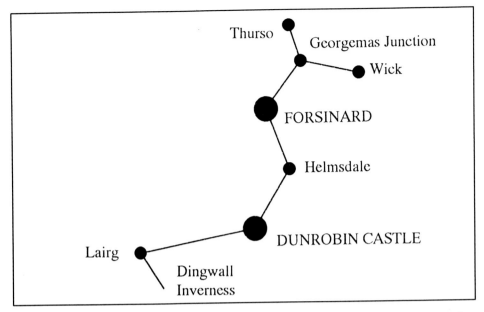

Georgemas Junction (three stops either side of Forsinard), but locations other than the town of Helmsdale have few, if any, facilities. Indeed, the stations at Kildonan, Kinbrace, Altnabreac and Scotscalder are as isolated as Forsinard. The coastline around Dunrobin Castle (immediately South of Brora, but with a station only open during the Summer) has a wider range of species, being nearer woodland and cover. Buzzard, merlin, and Scottish Crossbill may all be seen here.

Birdwatching in this part of Scotland is probably most pleasurable from the train, since the birds ignore the train, and one can remain warm and dry, difficult elsewhere in this barren but beautiful landscape.

Notes:

Probably Britain's most comical bird, the Puffin is generally found around the rocky shores of the North and West. As can be seen, this burrow-nesting seabird is a fish-eater and, with these markings, easily identified. Although the shape of the Pheasant is familiar, colours vary considerably. The bird shown here has the most common colourings, but green birds are known, whilst the females are a nondescript speckled light brown. Pheasants are to be found in most of Britain's arable farmland areas, preferring to run rather than fly away from trouble. [J.H.Hume; N.G. Harris

The Greylag goose is the largest of the grey geese to be seen in Britain, and is widespread. However, most of the birds seen are re-introductions, and the genuinely native stock is only to be found in North-West Scotland, a far cry from the London park where this one was seen feeding. Although the House Sparrow is probably the most familiar of all British birds, it is not the most common, as it is mostly found only around human habitation. Elsewhere, care must be taken to look for other 'little brown jobs', as the house sparrow is easily mistaken for the tree sparrow, dunnock, skylark, linnet or members of the bunting family. Sound is a useful clue – all the other species can sing properly, whilst the house sparrow can only chirp. [N.G. Harris (2)

59

FRODSHAM MARSHES

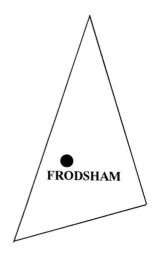

FRODSHAM

County:	Cheshire.
Map:	Sheet 117 ref. SJ510780.
Nearest Stations:	Frodsham, Helsby.
Distance (m):	200-500, depending on station.
Timetable nos.:	83; 107.
Rail Service:	Hourly service from Manchester Victoria via Warrington Bank Quay and Runcorn East to Llandudno via Chester, Rhyl and Llandudno Junction. Helsby also served by half-hourly shuttle service to Hooton via Ellesmere Port. *Time taken:* Runcorn 8 mins, Ellesmere Port 9 mins, Chester 12 mins, Warrington 15 mins, Hooton 18 mins, Manchester 47 mins, Rhyl 60 mins, Llandudno 90 mins. *Sundays:* No Hooton-Helsby service. *Connections* available at Hooton for Birkenhead and Liverpool; at Chester for Wrexham, Shrewsbury and Crewe; at Warrington for Wigan and Preston; at Manchester for Bolton, Rochdale and Metrolink services to Bury and Altrincham, and at Llandudno Junction for Holyhead and Blaenau Ffestiniog.
Local Facilities:	Local shops and pubs; general information centre at Frodsham.
Habitat:	Farmland, sludge beds, rough grazing.

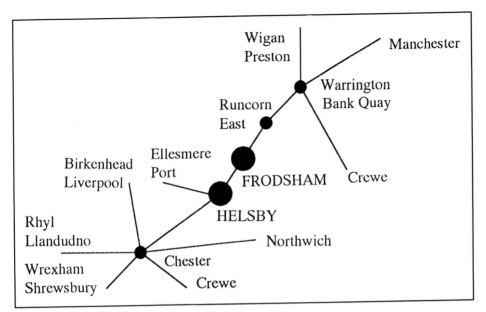

Access: Access to the marshes is from lanes off to the West of the main A56 road, South of Frodsham but North of Helsby stations.

Likely Sightings: Wildfowl (e.g. wigeon); waders (especially on passage); short-eared owl; hen harrier.

Best Time of Year: Winter, for wildfowl.

Notes:

HAMPSTEAD HEATH

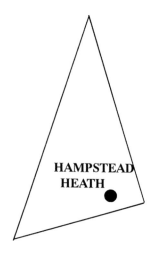

HAMPSTEAD HEATH

County:	London.
Map:	Sheet 176 ref. TO270865.
Nearest Stations:	Hampstead Heath, Gospel Oak; Hampstead (LUL).
Distance (m):	100-500, depending on station.
Timetable nos.:	58,2; Northern Line.
Rail Service:	Hampstead Heath and Gospel Oak: 20 minute frequency service from Richmond via Willesden Junction and West Hampstead to North Woolwich via Highbury, Stratford and West Ham (the "North London Line"). Gospel Oak also served by half-hourly service to Barking via Harringay Green Lanes and Leytonstone High Road. Hampstead LUL served by Northern Line trains from Edgware to Morden via Camden Town and Euston and either Charing Cross or Bank.

Time taken: West Hampstead 5 mins, Euston 10 mins, Stratford 24 mins, Richmond 28 mins, Barking 34 mins, North Woolwich 39 mins.

Sundays: No Winter service (October-mid May).

Connections available at West Hampstead for St Albans, Luton, Bromley and the Jubilee line; at Willesden Junc. for Wembley and Harrow; at Richmond for Twickenham, Kingston and Staines; at Highbury for the Victoria line; at

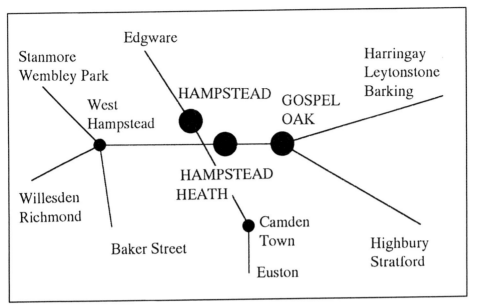

Edgware
Stanmore
Wembley Park
West
Hampstead
HAMPSTEAD
GOSPEL
OAK
Harringay
Leytonstone
Barking
Willesden
Richmond
HAMPSTEAD
HEATH
Camden
Town
Baker Street
Euston
Highbury
Stratford

Stratford for Ilford, Romford, the Docklands Light Railway and the Central line, and at West Ham for the District line. In addition, the Northern line intersects eight of the other underground lines in Central London, as well as serving Euston, King's Cross, Charing Cross, Waterloo and London Bridge main line termini.

Local Facilities: Parades of shops may be found adjacent to the two Hampstead stations.

Habitat: Parkland and woodland, including ponds.

Access: Access to the Heath is easy from a number of streets, including Parliament Hill, adjacent to Hampstead Heath station.

Likely Sightings: Tits, nuthatch, jay, woodpeckers; kestrel; moorhen, coot, water rail.

Best Time of Year: Quite profitable in Winter when reduced vegetation forces some species to make themselves more obvious.

Notes:

HAYLE ESTUARY

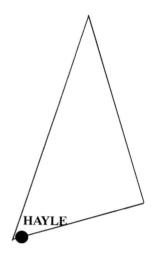

HAYLE

County:	Cornwall .
Map:	Sheet 203 ref. SW547364.
Nearest Stations:	Hayle, Lelant, Lelant Saltings.
Distance (m):	0-1000, depending on station.
Timetable nos.:	135, 144.
Rail Service:	Hayle: 11 trains per day from Penzance via St Erth to Plymouth via Truro; some services are extended beyond Plymouth to Bristol or London Paddington via Exeter.

Lelant: Irregular hourly service between St Erth and St Ives; some services extended beyond St Erth to Penzance. More frequent in the Summer.

Lelant Saltings: Five trains per day in Winter, but more-than-hourly service in Summer on the St Ives branch; the station serves a large "park-and-ride" car park designed to keep tourist cars out of St Ives.

Time taken: St Erth 4 mins, St Ives 10 mins, Penzance 12 mins, Truro 26 mins, Plymouth 1 hour 50 mins.

Sundays: No Winter service (October-mid May) on St Ives branch; limited service at Hayle.

Connections available at Truro for Falmouth; at Plymouth for Gunnislake, Newton Abbot and Exeter. Boat and helicopter services from Penzance to the Scilly Isles.

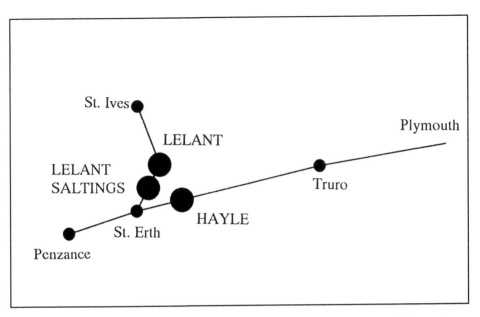

Local Facilities:	Old Quay House Inn near Lelant Saltings; local shops in Hayle.
Habitat:	Estuary and lagoon; also small wood near Lelant station.
Access:	Access to the lagoon is off the B3301, from which excellent views of the estuary may be had, the best spot perhaps being where the River Hayle passes under the road.
Likely Sightings:	Waders in large quantities and many varieties (e.g. dunlin, plovers, bar-tailed godwit), gulls, ducks; rock pipit, tits, finches etc. in the numerous gorse bushes surrounding the lagoon.
Best Time of Year:	Good all year, but probably better outside the main holiday season, when excessive traffic is a nuisance.
Notes:	

HILLBRE ISLANDS

County:	Merseyside.
Map:	Sheet 108 ref. SJ185882.
Nearest Stations:	West Kirby.
Distance (m):	500 plus up to 3km across the sand.
Timetable nos.:	104.
Rail Service:	15 minute frequency service from Liverpool via Birkenhead and Bidston. Note that trains run clockwise only around the Central Liverpool section, always serving Moorfields, then Lime Street, then Central. *Time taken:* Bidston 14 mins, Birkenhead 23 mins, Liverpool 29 mins. *Connections* available at Bidston for Neston and Wrexham; at Birkenhead North for New Brighton; at Birkenhead Hamilton Square for Chester and Ellesmere Port; at Liverpool Lime Street for Wigan, St Helens, Warrington, Manchester and Runcorn; and at Liverpool Moorfields/ Central for Formby, Southport, Ormskirk, Kirkby and Hunt's Cross.
Local Facilities:	Local shops and pubs in this day-tripper resort.
Habitat:	Offshore island and sandbanks.
Access:	Turn right outside the station, and make straight for the beach (200m). Access to the two Hillbre Islands is across

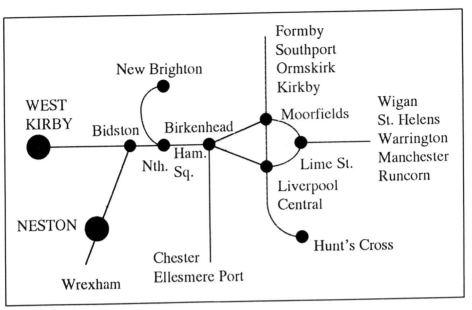

	the sand exposed at low tide (at least two hours either side of low water).
Likely Sightings:	Waders (e.g. greenshank, sandpipers); wildfowl; gulls; rock pipit.
Best Time of Year:	Spring and Autumn migratory periods.
Nearby Sites:	Neston, on the Bidston-Wrexham line, gives easy access (1000m) along minor roads to the West of the station to mudflats, important for ducks (e.g. pintail) and birds of prey (in Winter) as well as waders at low tide (at high tide, the waders roost at Hillbre).

Notes:

JUMBLES RESERVOIR

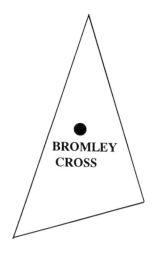

BROMLEY
CROSS

County: Greater Manchester/Lancashire.
Map: Sheet 109 ref. SD735138.
Nearest Station: Bromley Cross.
Distance (m): 800.
Timetable no.: 95.
Rail Service: Hourly service from Rochdale via Manchester Victoria, Salford and Bolton to Blackburn.
Time taken: Bolton 7 mins, Blackburn 23 mins, Manchester 32 mins, Rochdale 62 mins.
Sundays: Services terminate at Manchester.
Connections available at Blackburn for Burnley and Colne, at Bolton for Wigan, Preston and Stockport, and at Manchester for St Helens, Warrington, Liverpool, Todmorden and Halifax (also Metrolink services to Bury and Altrincham).
Local Facilities: Toilets.
Habitat: Reservoir, pasture and woods.
Access: From a track running North-East from, and parallel to, the railway.
Likely Sightings: Varied, including Grest Crested Grebe; waders e.g. Snipe, Common Sandpiper.

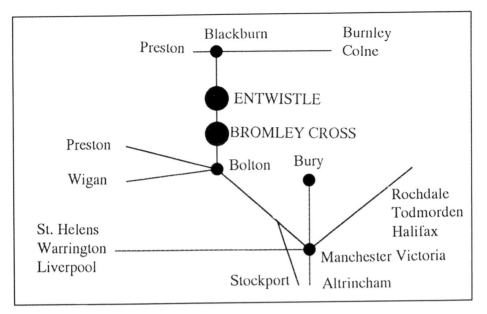

Preston — Blackburn

Burnley
Colne

ENTWISTLE

BROMLEY CROSS

Preston

Wigan

Bolton   Bury

Rochdale
Todmorden
Halifax

St. Helens
Warrington
Liverpool

Manchester Victoria

Stockport

Altrincham

Best Time of Year: Winter, when ducks usually appear in greater numbers.
Nearby Sites: Entwistle (one stop, or 5 mins) to the North gives access,
                   past a pub, to Turton and Wayoh reservoirs.
Notes:

The Black-headed Gull has adapted its lifestyle to fit in with people, and is frequently seen, in towns, at reservoirs and in agricultural areas. This example, however, was photographed in Scotland in something rather more akin to its natural surroundings. [N.G. Harris

KENNET VALLEY

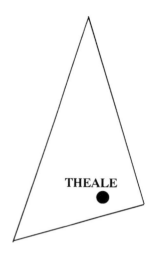

THEALE
●

County:	Berkshire.
Map:	Sheet 175 ref. SU647705.
Nearest Station:	Theale.
Distance (m):	500.
Timetable no.:	116.
Rail Service:	Two-hourly stopping services between Reading and Newbury (with some continuing to Bedwyn) alternate with fast services from Newbury to London Paddington via Reading, giving an hourly service overall.
	Time taken: Reading 10 mins, Newbury 23 mins, London 42 mins.
	Sundays: Limited-stop services between Reading and Newbury.
	Connections available at Reading for Didcot, Swindon, Oxford, Maidenhead, Slough, Wokingham, Bracknell, Guildford and Basingstoke. (Note that changing at Reading West for Basingstoke can be preferable at certain times of day).
Local Facilities:	Local shops and public house only.
Habitat:	River/canal-bank, gravel pits.
Access:	Turn left (South) outside the station. Access from footpaths either side of the road immediately beyond the Kennet and

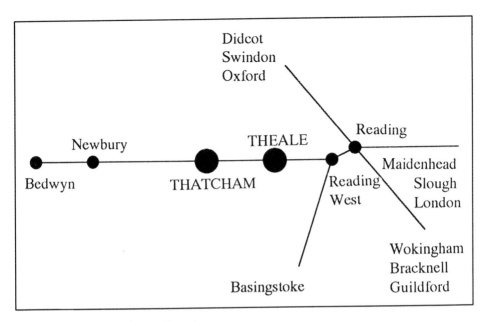

	Avon Canal.
Likely Sightings:	Diving ducks (e.g. pochard, tufted duck), great crested grebe; warblers, tits; waders (e.g. snipe).
Best Time of Year:	Winter, when waders usually appear in greater numbers.
Nearby Sites:	Similar gravel workings at Thatcham have reed beds, with reed and sedge warblers present. Thatcham is 10 - 15 mins West of Theale (i.e. nearer Newbury), and is also served by the fast trains.
Notes:	

KINGHORN

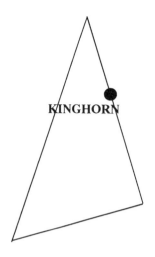

County:	Fife.
Map:	Sheet 66 ref. NT270868.
Nearest Stations:	Kinghorn.
Distance (m):	500.
Timetable nos.:	241.
Rail Service:	Hourly circular service from Edinburgh, Haymarket and Inverkeithing to Kirkcaldy, returning to Edinburgh via Dunfermline and Inverkeithing.
	Evenings: Hourly service Edinburgh - Dundee.
	Sundays: Joint hourly service of alternate circular and Dundee trains.
	Time taken: Kirkcaldy 6 mins, Inverkeithing 15 mins, Edinburgh 38 mins, Dunfermline 40 mins, Dundee 50 mins.
	Connections available at Kirkcaldy for Perth, Dundee and Aberdeen, at Haymarket for Glasgow, Bathgate, Falkirk and Shotts, and at Edinburgh for North Berwick and InterCity services to Newcastle and Carlisle.
Local Facilities:	Local shops only.
Habitat:	Muddy beach and rocky coastline.
Access:	Access to the mudflats is via Pettycur harbour, 500m to the South of the station, whilst the rocky coastline is to the

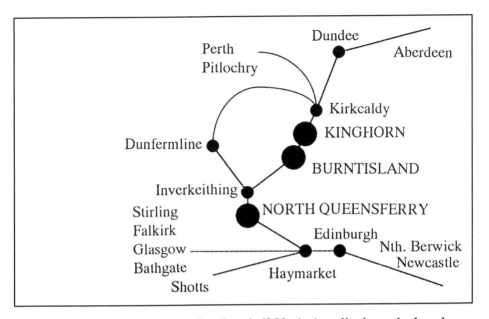

North, past the church (250m). A walk along the beach leads to Burntisland (4km), the next station further South.

Likely Sightings: Sea ducks e.g. eider, red-breasted merganser; waders including bar-tailed godwit; gulls; cormorant; gannet; rock pipit.

Best Time of Year: Autumn for passage waders.

Nearby Sites: North Queensferry, one stop South of Inverkeithing, has a little harbour, in which gulls and waders may be seen, whilst it also provides a good vantage point from which to observe birds in the Forth Estuary.

Notes:

LEIGHTON MOSS

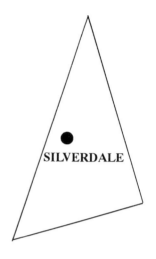

SILVERDALE

County: Lancashire.
Map: Sheet 97 ref. SD480752.
Nearest Station: Silverdale.
Distance (m):   400.
Timetable no.:   110.
Rail Service: Approximately hourly service from Barrow-in-Furness via
                   Grange-over-Sands to Preston via Carnforth and Lancaster.
                   Some services extended beyond Preston to Bolton and
                   Manchester Victoria.
                   Time taken: Carnforth 8 mins, Grange 10 mins, Lancaster
                   15 mins, Preston 37 mins, Barrow 46 mins.
                   Connections available at Carnforth for Skipton and Leeds;
                   at Barrow for Millom and Whitehaven; at Lancaster for
                   Carlisle; and at Preston for Blackburn, Burnley, Wigan, St
                   Helens and Liverpool.
Local Facilities: RSPB information centre, shop and tea-shop at the reserve.
Habitat: Reedswamp and surrounding woods.
Access: Turn left (North-East) outside the station; access to the
                   main part of the reserve is off to the right. Additionally
                   waders and gulls may be seen from the public footpath
                   leading Westwards from Crag Foot, some 1500m South of
                   the station.

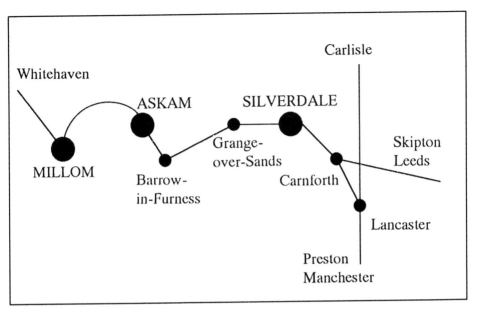

Likely Sightings: Warblers (e.g. reed, sedge, grasshopper); ducks; bearded tit; bittern; hen harrier; waders, gulls; redstart and pied flycatcher in the woods.

Best Time of Year: The Winter for ducks and waders or the woods in Summer for warblers etc.

Nearby Sites: To the West of Barrow, the line to Whitehaven follows the Duddon estuary closely. Every station between Askam and Millom has close, if not immediate, access to the estuary, with its waders. Although there are no facilities at Green Road, Millom is a small town, and Foxfield, Kirkby-in-Furness and Askam are all villages with pubs.

Notes:

LOCH LOMOND

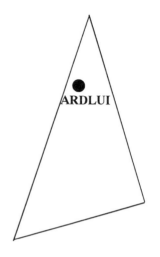

ARDLUI

County:	Strathclyde.
Map:	Sheet 56 ref. NS358582.
Nearest Stations:	Ardlui.
Distance (m):	200.
Timetable nos.:	227.
Rail Service:	Four trains per day from Glasgow Queen Street via Dumbarton and Helensburgh Upper to Oban/Fort William and Mallaig, splitting at Crianlarich. *Time taken:* Crianlarich 15 mins, Oban and Glasgow both 1 hour 40 mins, Fort William 2 hours, Mallaig 3 hours 40 mins. *Connections* available at Dumbarton Central for local stations to Airdrie, Hamilton and Motherwell; and at Glasgow for Cumbernauld and Edinburgh.
Local Facilities:	Hotel, toilets and campsite.
Habitat:	Loch, woodland and crag.
Access:	Take the pedestrian ferry (Summer only) from the pier almost opposite the station to the Eastern bank of Loch Lomond, and explore both Northwards and Southwards using the West Highland Way long-distance footpath.
Likely Sightings:	Ducks e.g. red-breasted merganser; redstart, wagtails, warblers; peregrine on crags; grouse family including

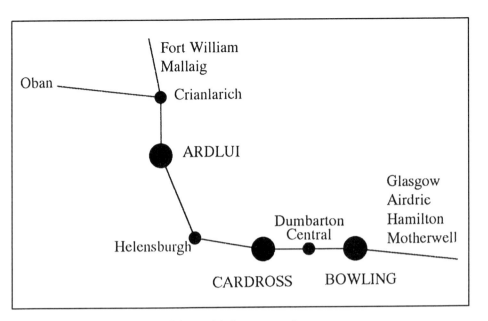

capercaillie on higher ground.

Best Time of Year: Summer.

Nearby Sites: Cardross and Bowling (respectively two stops West and East of Dumbarton Central, on the suburban network) give immediate access to the Northern shore of the River Clyde, with its waders (e.g. curlew), gulls and terns.

Notes:

LOCHWINNOCH

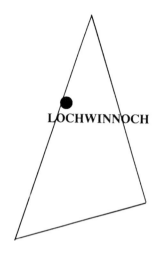

LOCHWINNOCH

County:	Strathclyde.
Map:	Sheet 63 ref. NS358582.
Nearest Stations:	Lochwinnoch.
Distance (m):	200.
Timetable nos.:	221.
Rail Service:	Hourly service from Glasgow Central via Paisley Gilmour Street and Johnstone to Ardrossan Town (qv) via Kilwinning.
	Time taken: Johnstone 8 mins, Paisley 12 mins, Kilwinning 13 mins, Glasgow 22 mins, Ardrossan 26 mins.
	Connections available at Paisley for Gourock and Greenock, at Kilwinning for Ayr and Largs, and at Glasgow for suburban services to Motherwell, Hamilton, Cathcart and Dalmuir.
Local Facilities:	An RSPB information centre and shop (closed Thursdays).
Habitat:	Barr Loch, marsh and scrub.
Access:	Access to the reserve is safest following the station approach road, which meets the main A760 opposite the reserve entrance.
Likely Sightings:	Ducks; waders including greenshank and whimbrel on passage, gulls, Great Crested grebe; tits and warblers (sedge and grasshopper).

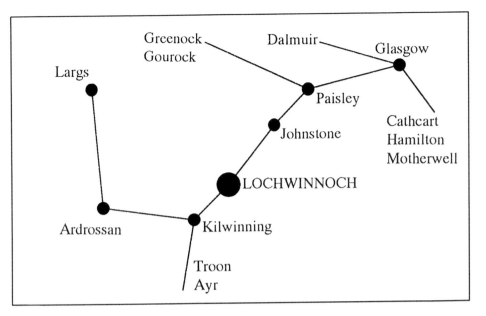

Best Time of Year: Autumn for passage waders.

Notes:

The Moorhen is a waterside bird, feeding in reeds and marshes, but also on more open grassland where this is adjacent. [N.G. Harris

LONGCROSS

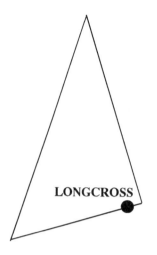

LONGCROSS

County:	Surrey.
Map:	Sheet 175 ref. SU978660.
Nearest Station:	Longcross.
Distance (m):	0 (footbridge gives good views of woods).
Timetable no.:	150.
Rail Service:	Hourly service from Waterloo via Clapham Junction, Richmond and Staines to Guildford via Ascot and Aldershot.

Time taken: Ascot 8 mins, Staines 13 mins, Richmond 27 mins, Clapham Junction 35 mins, Aldershot 38 mins, Waterloo 42 mins, Guildford 61 mins.

Peaks: Some additional Waterloo-Reading services stop.

Sundays: No service.

Connections available at Virginia Water for Chertsey and Woking (these trains also serve Hounslow via Staines); at Ascot for Bracknell and Reading; at Aldershot for Farnham; at Staines for Windsor and Hounslow; at Richmond for Kingston, Willesden and LUL's District line; at Guildford for Haslemere and Dorking; at Clapham Junction for Wimbledon and Croydon.

Local Facilities:	None.
Habitat:	Woods (at end of golf course), heath.

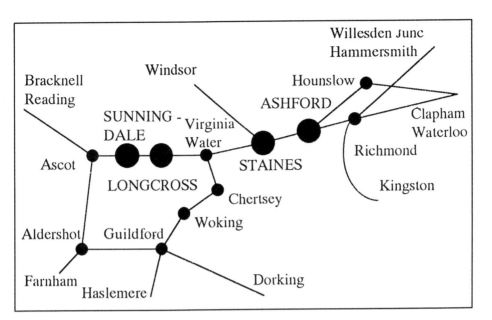

Access: Access (pedestrian only) is by a track direct from the platform across the heath, skirting the MoD installation.

Likely Sightings: Warblers, chats; tits, goldcrest; sparrowhawk.

Best Time of Year: Early Summer (to maximise possible Sightings of small migrants).

Nearby Sites: A 3km walk to Sunningdale across Chobham Common is likely to increase the number of species seen; Sunningdale has better facilities and a better train service (including trains on Sundays).

The two Staines reservoirs are bisected by a footpath reached at its Western end by the A3044 from Staines, and at its Eastern end by the B378 from Ashford, both 1500m away form the respective stations. These reservoirs are renowned for interesting waders in addition to their duck populations.

Notes:

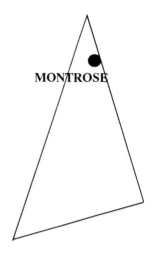

MONTROSE

MONTROSE BASIN

County:	Tayside.
Map:	Sheet 54 ref. NO712580.
Nearest Station:	Montrose.
Distance (m):	0 (Mudflats visible from platform).
Timetable no.:	229.
Rail Service:	Irregular hourly service from Aberdeen to Edinburgh via Arbroath, Dundee and Kirkcaldy; three per day are InterCity services to London King's Cross via Newcastle. Most Glasgow Queen Street-Stirling-Perth-Aberdeen trains also stop (10 per day).
	Time taken: Arbroath 16 mins, Dundee 32 mins, Aberdeen 43 mins, Perth 55 mins, Kirkcaldy 75 mins, Stirling 90 mins, Edinburgh 108 mins, Glasgow 2 hours.
	Connections available at Aberdeen for Elgin and Inverness; at Dundee for local stations to Edinburgh; at Perth for Pitlochry; at Stirling for Falkirk.
Local Facilities:	Montrose is a sizeable town with all the shopping and accommodation facilities one would expect.
Habitat:	Tidal estuarine mudflats.
Access:	Access to the mudflats is surprisingly difficult except for views from the station platform (and footbridge, if extra height is required); however, these views are excellent,

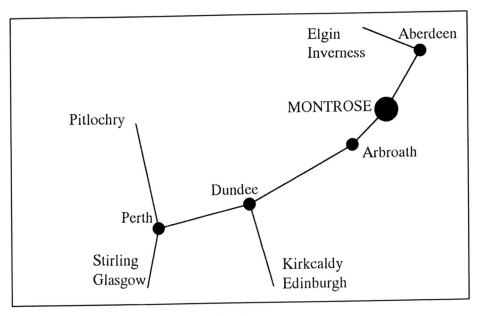

especially at high tide.

Likely Sightings: Waders (of many varieties, and in large quantities, but especially the Calidris family), gulls, cormorant.

Best Time of Year: The state of the tide is probably more important than the time of year, since at low tide birds are too far away to be easily identified. However, Spring and Autumn may bring rarities on migration.

Notes:

NEW FOREST

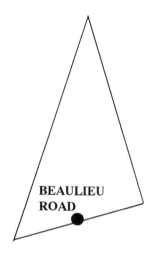

BEAULIEU ROAD

County:	Hampshire.
Map:	Sheet 196 ref. SU350064.
Nearest Station:	Beaulieu Road.
Distance (m):	0 (the station is in the middle of heathland).
Timetable no.:	158.
Rail Service:	Hourly service from Portsmouth via Fareham and Southampton to Wareham via Brockenhurst, Bournemouth and Poole.
	Time taken: Brockenhurst 6 mins, Southampton 16 mins, Bournemouth 47 mins, Fareham 48 mins, Poole 59 mins, Portsmouth 70 mins, Wareham 73 mins.
	Sundays: Hourly slow Bournemouth London Waterloo service.
	Connections available at Brockenhurst for Weymouth, and at Southampton for Salisbury, Winchester, Basingstoke, Portsmouth, Havant and Chichester.
Local Facilities:	Pub/hotel 50m from the station. Camping site 2km on other side of railway.
Habitat:	Woods, heath, scrub.
Access:	Several footpaths lead onto the heath within 200m of the station entrance.
Likely Sightings:	Warblers (including Dartford), chats, woodlark; waders e.g.

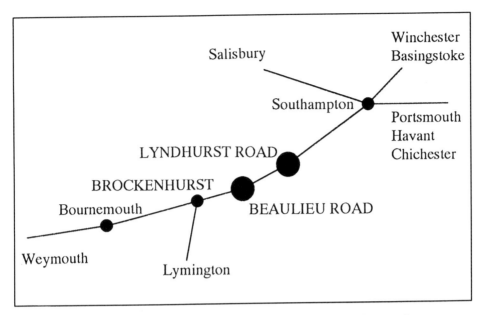

Winchester
Basingstoke

Salisbury

Southampton

Portsmouth
Havant
Chichester

LYNDHURST ROAD

BROCKENHURST

Bournemouth

BEAULIEU ROAD

Weymouth

Lymington

Curlew and Woodcock; Nightjar, owls; Buzzard.

Best Time of Year: Summer evenings (for Nightjar, Woodcock and owls). Unfortunately, there are at present no trains stopping in the evenings, so one must either stay at the hotel, camp, or (if fit and adventurous) walk the 8km to Brockenhurst through the woods in the dark.

Nearby Sites: The next station towards Southampton (which is Lyndhurst Road) offers good woodland watching.

Notes:

PEAK DISTRICT (NORTH)

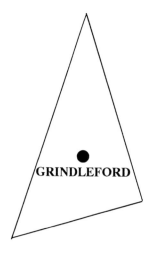

GRINDLEFORD

County: Derbyshire.
Map: Sheet 119 ref.SK252787.
Best Station: Grindleford.
Distance (m):   100.
Timetable nos.:   90.
Rail Service: Hourly slow service from Manchester Piccadilly via New
                  Mills Central to Doncaster via Sheffield and Meadowhall.
                  Time taken: Sheffield 17 mins, New Mills 35 mins,
                  Romiley 44 mins, Doncaster 45 - 65 mins (depending on
                  the wait at Sheffield), Manchester 61 mins.
                  Connections available at Sheffield for Chesterfield,
                  Rotherham, Barnsley, Wakefield and Leeds; at Doncaster
                  for York, Goole and Hull, at Romiley for Hyde, and at
                  Manchester for Stockport, Warrington, Bolton and Preston
                  by mainline services, and Altrincham and Bury by
                  Metrolink. Supertram services should link Sheffield and
                  Meadowhall stations with other parts of Sheffield from
                  1994.
Local Facilities: A few scattered pubs and hotels.
Access: Footpaths lead straight from the station access road through
                  the woods into the moorland beyond.
Habitat: Woods, farmland, moors.

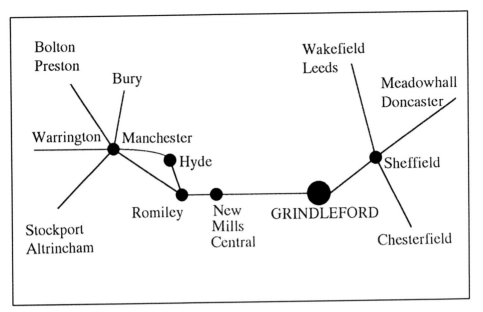

Likely Sightings: Warblers, woodpeckers, redstart, tits in the woods; skylark, lapwing, corn bunting on farmed slopes; red grouse, meadow pipit, twite, curlew, golden plover on the moors. Watch for dippers and wagtails in the streams, and for birds of prey—especially around the rocky outcrops.

Best Time of Year: Early Summer (but preferably away from peak holiday periods); Winter conditions can be bleak.

Nearby Sites: All the other stations on the "Hope Valley" line as far West as Chinley offer access to the moors of the Peak District but, in general, the distance from the station is greater than at Grindleford, and there is less woodland elsewhere. Edale is, of course, famous for being the start of the Pennine Way.

Notes:

PEAK DISTRICT (SOUTH)

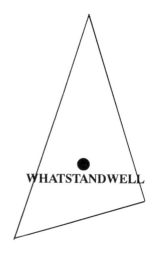

WHATSTANDWELL

County:	Derbyshire.
Map:	Sheet 119 ref. SK333545.
Nearest Station:	Whatstandwell.
Distance (m):	200.
Timetable no.:	54.
Rail Service:	About ten trains per day from Derby to Matlock.
	Time taken: Matlock 10 mins, Derby 21 mins.
	Connections available at Derby for Stoke, Uttoxeter, Burton, Tamworth, Birmingham, Chesterfield, Sheffield, Nottingham, Loughborough and Leicester.
Local Facilities:	Public house.
Access:	The canalside footpath runs parallel to the railway at this point; access can be gained from the road overbridge immediately to the North of the station. For the woods, cross the railway and the canal, then bear left up the minor road to Holloway. Footpaths lead from this road through the woods.
Habitat:	River/canalside, woods, farmland.
Likely Sightings:	Warblers, woodpeckers, redstart, tits in the woods; skylark, lapwing, corn bunting on farmed slopes; ducks, swans in the river/canal.
Best Time of Year:	Early Summer, for warblers.

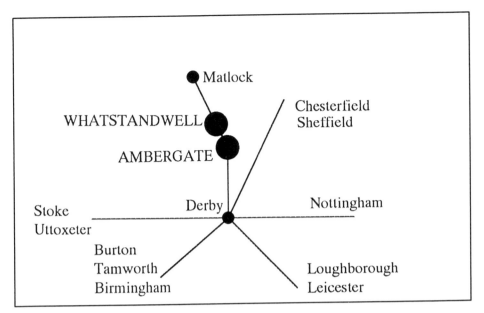

Nearby Sites: Similar woodland walks may be had from Ambergate (one
                  stop further South) .

Notes:

PENARTH FLATS

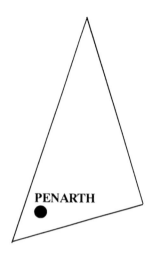

PENARTH

County:	South Glamorgan.
Map:	Sheet 171 ref. ST185726.
Nearest Stations:	Cogan, Dingle Road and Penarth.
Distance (m):	200-800.
Timetable no.:	130 .
Rail Service:	Trains every 20 minutes as part of the Cardiff suburban network. Cogan lies on the Barry branch, with services via Cardiff (Central and Queen Street stations) to Aberdare and Treherbert via Pontypridd, and Bargoed via Caerphilly. Dingle Road is on the Penarth branch, with services via Cardiff to Merthyr Tydfil and Treherbert via Pontypridd, and Rhymney via Caerphilly and Bargoed. *Time taken:* Cardiff Central 10 mins, Caerphilly 28 mins, Pontypridd 37 mins, Aberdare 60 mins, Merthyr 60 mins, Rhymney 65 mins and Treherbert 70 mins. *Connections* available at Cardiff Central for Newport, Cwmbran, Hereford, Gloucester, Bristol and Swansea, and for local services to Coryton and Radyr (also Maesteg from Autumn 1992).
Local Facilities:	Local shops in Penarth.
Access:	By public roads North of Cogan and Dingle Road, and East of Penarth, to the docks and shore respectively.

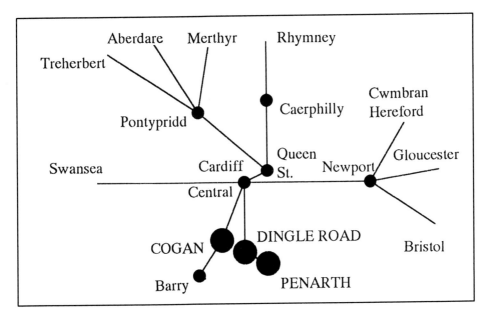

Habitat: Mudflats.
Likely Sightings: Waders (especially dunlin, knot and plovers); gulls.
Best Time of Year: Autumn may bring warblers, chats and rarities on
                     migration, and also shearwaters and skuas in from the open
                     sea.
Notes:

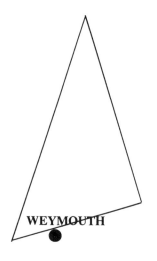

RADIPOLE LAKE

County:	Dorset.
Map:	Sheet 194 ref. SY676795.
Nearest Station:	Weymouth.
Distance (m):	200.
Timetable nos.:	123, 158.
Rail Service:	Hourly service from London Waterloo via Southampton, Bournemouth, Poole, Wareham and Dorchester South. Also irregular two-hourly service from Bristol via Bath, Westbury, Yeovil Pen Mill and Dorchester West.

Time taken: Dorchester 12 mins, Wareham 32 mins, Yeovil 43 mins, Poole 45 mins, Bournemouth 55 mins, Westbury 84 mins, Southampton 88 mins, Bath 1hr 52 mins, Bristol 2hrs 11 mins and Waterloo 2hrs 40 mins.

Connections available at Southampton for Salisbury, Winchester, Basingstoke, Havant and Chichester.

Local Facilities:	RSPB information centre with shop; public toilets in adjacent car park. Full range of shops, market and beach within 400m of station, also hotels and guest houses in this resort town.
Access:	Through the car park adjacent to, and West of, the station.
Habitat:	Reedbeds and scrub.
Likely Sightings:	Warblers (including Cetti's, reed, sedge and grasshopper),

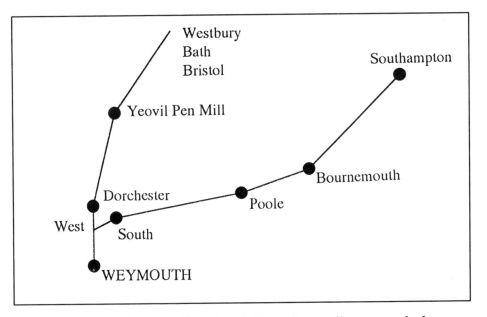

tits (including Bearded); waders; gulls; swans, ducks, grebes.

Best Time of Year: Early Summer (for the warblers).

Notes:

RYE HOUSE MARSH

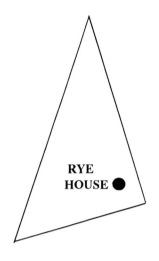

RYE
HOUSE ●

County:	Hertfordshire.
Map:	Sheet 166 ref. TL386100.
Nearest Station:	Rye House.
Distance (m):	300.
Timetable no.:	21.
Rail Service:	Half-hourly service from London Liverpool Street via Seven Sisters and Broxbourne to Hertford East. *Time taken:* Broxbourne 4 mins, Hertford 14 mins, Seven Sisters 29 mins, Liverpool Street 43 mins. *Peaks:* Some services to Stratford via Tottenham Hale. *Sundays:* Hourly shuttle Hertford East-Broxbourne. *Connections* available at Broxbourne for Waltham Cross, Bishops Stortford and Cambridge, at Seven Sisters for LUL's Victoria line, and at Liverpool Street for Ilford, Romford, Colchester and Southend Victoria, also other LUL services.
Local Facilities:	Pub near the station. Several hides on the reserve.
Habitat:	Marsh, lakes, woods.
Access:	Off minor lane to North of station.
Likely Sightings:	Ducks (particularly teal), waders (especially snipe); cormorant; reed and sedge warblers, finches; kingfisher; terns.

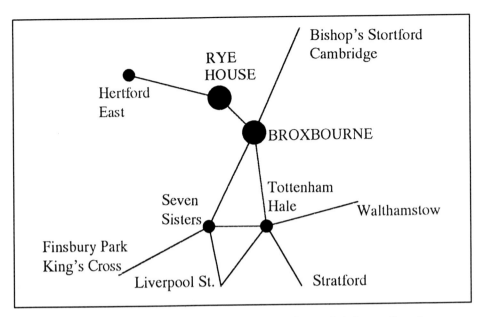

Best Time of Year: A year-round reserve with Winter sightings of waders, finches and buntings balanced against warblers and hirundines in the Summer. Interesting waders also occur on migration in the Spring and Autumn.

Nearby Sites: The Lea valley (in which Rye House lies) is generally quite good, and is traversed by a public footpath well into inner London. Even the short 6km walk to Broxbourne is worthwhile in terms of increasing the numbers of species seen, and the likelihood of seeing a kingfisher or two.

Notes:

ST BEES HEAD

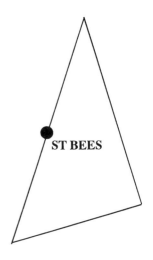

ST BEES

County: Cumbria.
Map: Sheet 89 ref. NX961118.
Nearest Station: St Bees.
Distance (m):   800.
Timetable no.:   113.
Rail Service: Four trains per day between Carlisle via Workington and
                 Whitehaven and Barrow-in-Furness via Ravenglass and
                 Millom.
                 Time taken: Whitehaven 10 mins, Ravenglass 24 mins,
                 Workington 28 mins, Millom 47 mins, Barrow 76 mins,
                 Carlisle 82 mins.
                 Sundays: No service.
                 Connections at Carlisle for Dumfries, Motherwell,
                 Glasgow, Edinburgh, Hexham and Newcastle, and at
                 Barrow for Lancaster, Preston and Manchester Victoria.
Local Facilities: Toilets.
Habitat: Sandstone cliffs, grassland and gorse.
Access: Off lane to West of station.
Likely Sightings: Seabirds (e.g. guillemot, black guillemot, kittiwake,
                 razorbill, puffin, fulmar, cormorant, shag, gannet, skuas,
                 shearwaters, terns, gulls); raven; stonechat; rock pipit;
                 kestrel, peregrine.

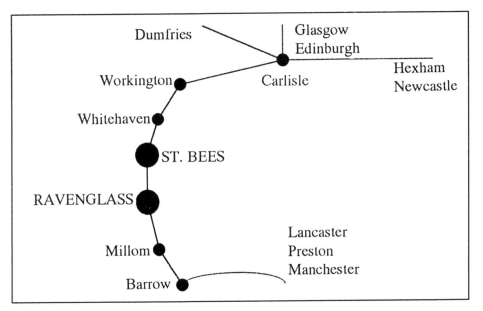

Best Time of Year: Early Summer, for breeding guillemot, puffin etc.; Autumn for shearwaters and skuas on migration.

Nearby Sites: Ravenglass station is within 200m of the main street in this village with pub and information centre; the nature reserve on the other side of the Esk estuary is easily viewed. The reserve is known for its exceptionally large colony of breeding black-headed gulls.

Notes:

SANDWELL VALLEY

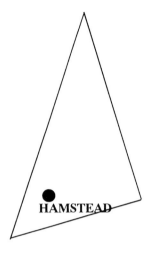

HAMSTEAD

County:	West Midlands.
Map:	Sheet 139 ref. SP035926.
Nearest Station:	Hamstead.
Distance (m):	1500.
Timetable no.:	70.
Rail Service:	Half-hourly service between Wallsall and Birmingham New Street via Aston.
	Time taken: Wallsall 10 mins, Birmingham 13 mins.
	Sundays: No service.
	Connections at Wallsall for Hednesford; at Aston for Sutton Coldfield and Lichfield City; and at Birmingham for Smethwick, Wolverhampton, Stourbridge, Kidderminster, Longbridge, Coventry, and Leicester.
Local Facilities:	Parade of shops near the station; an Information Centre (closed on Thursdays) at the reserve.
Habitat:	Very mixed, including wooded and open country, and a lake in a bend of the River Tame.
Access:	Walk (or take the number 16 bus) down Hamstead Road, North-West of the station; turn left at Hamstead School into Tanhouse Avenue, part of a housing estate, then left again over the railway.
Likely Sightings:	Tits, warblers and other woodland species; ducks, waders,

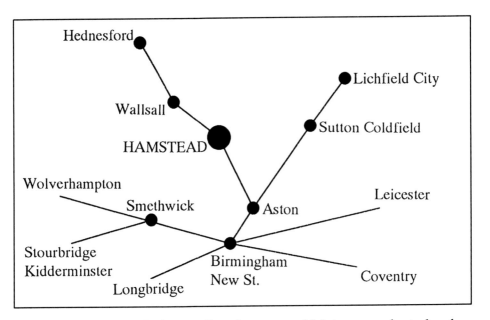

gulls, heron; Canada geese and Mute swans; kestrel and sparrowhawk. The wide range of habitats, together with the presence of an adjoining golf course, leads to a wide range of species.

Best Time of Year: Late Spring, when migrants have just arrived.

Notes:

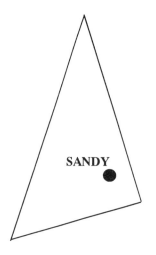

County:	Bedfordshire.
Map:	Sheet 153 ref. TL185480.
Nearest Station:	Sandy.
Distance (m):	500.
Timetable no.:	25.
Rail Service:	Half-hourly service from London King's Cross and Finsbury Park. One train per hour runs via Hertford North and Stevenage to Peterborough via Huntingdon, the other running direct via Stevenage only, and terminating at Huntingdon.

Time taken: Huntingdon 17 mins, Stevenage 20 mins, Hertford 32 mins, Peterborough 36 mins, King's Cross 46 mins (56 via Hertford) .

Connections available at Stevenage for Royston and Cambridge, at Hertford for local stations to Enfield, at Peterborough for Stamford, Leicester, March, and InterCity services to Grantham and the North, at Finsbury Park for LUL's Piccadilly and Victoria lines, and at King's Cross for Thameslink services to Luton and Croydon, also LUL's Northern, Metropolitan and Hammersmith & City lines.

Local Facilities: Pub only; Sandy's shops are away from the railway. RSPB shop, information centre and toilets at the Lodge.

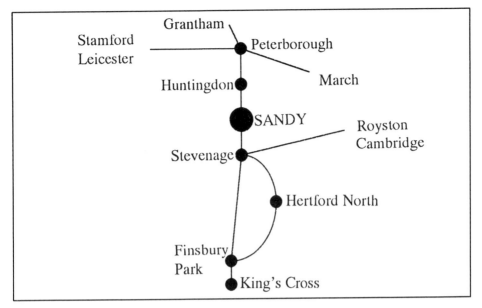

Habitat:	Farmland with flooded pit near the station, wood and heath around the Lodge.
Access:	Turn right and right again outside the station, into Stratford Road, running parallel to the railway. A circular walk of 5km may be had by following this as far as 193476, before turning Northwards through the grounds of the RSPB's Lodge headquarters, returning to the station along the B1042.
Likely Sightings:	Ducks may be seen in the pit visible across the railway just South of the station, with crows, yellowhammer and turtle dove in the adjoining fields, whilst Sandy Warren is good for a wide variety of tits and warblers, as well as finches and woodpeckers.
Best Time of Year:	Early Summer, for turtle dove and warblers.
Nearby Sites:	Turning South at grid ref. 193476 leads to Biggleswade Common, an excellent site for kestrel, corn bunting, meadow pipit etc.
Notes:	

SEVERN ESTUARY

SEVERN
BEACH

County: Avon.
Map: Sheet 172 ref. ST538847.
Nearest Station: Severn Beach.
Distance (m):   200.
Timetable no.:   133 .
Rail Service: Approximately hourly service from Bristol (Temple
                    Meads) via Stapleton Road and Avonmouth.
                    Time taken: Avonmouth 11 mins, Stapleton Road 33 mins,
                    Bristol 40 mins.
                    Sundays: No service.
                    Connections available at Stapleton Road for Yate and
                    Gloucester, and at Bristol for Weston-super-Mare, Taunton,
                    Bath, Westbury, Chippenham, Swindon, Newport and
                    Cardiff.
Local Facilities: Local shops only.
Habitat: Estuarine mudflats.
Access: Turn left outside the station; the lane leads immediately to
                    the shore.
Likely Sightings: Waders e.g. plovers, turnstone, redshank, curlew, dunlin,
                    knot, purple sandpiper, bar-tailed godwit.
Best Time of Year: Winter.
Nearby Sites: On the other side of the estuary, Caldicot and Severn

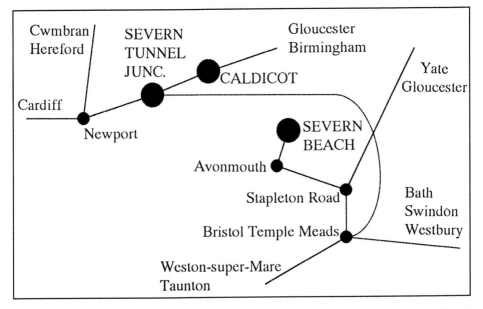

Tunnel Junction stations are within 200m of the marshland and rough grazing behind the river banks, which are easily reached on foot within 500 and 1200m respectively. Both stations are served by the two-hourly local service between Chepstow and Cardiff, but Caldicot is also served by two-hourly through services from Cardiff to Nottingham via Birmingham and Gloucester, whilst Cardiff - Portsmouth services via Bristol stop every two hours at Severn Tunnel Junction.

Notes:

SHIBDON POND

BLAYDON

County:	Tyne and Wear.
Map:	Sheet 88 ref. NZ195628.
Nearest Station:	Blaydon.
Distance (m):	1200.
Timetable no.:	48.
Rail Service:	Five trains per day each way between Newcastle and Hexham, with one train at lunchtime and the others in the peaks. Some of the Newcastle trains run through to Sunderland, whilst some of the Hexham services run through to Carlisle. *Time taken:* Newcastle 14 mins, Hexham 29 mins, Sunderland 41 mins, Carlisle 82 mins. *Sundays:* Four trains, times well-spaced. *Connections* available at Hexham for Carlisle and Dumfries, at Newcastle for Durham, Darlington, Morpeth, Sunderland and the Tyne and Wear Metro, and at Carlisle for Whitehaven and Workington.
Local Facilities:	A supermarket and other shops near the station; public toilets en route.
Habitat:	Subsidence pond, with swamp and scrub.
Access:	Cross the dual-carriageway by the footbridge, and then turn South-East along the B6317. The reserve (with nature trail)

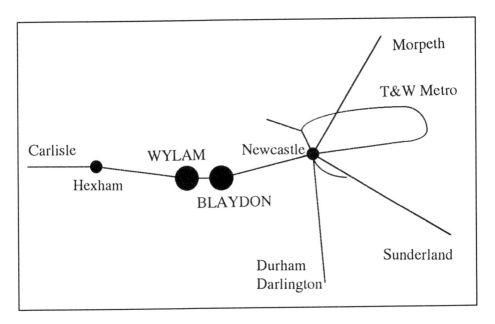

	is on the left.
Likely Sightings:	Wildfowl (often several hundred), heron; many other miscellaneous species (over 160 recorded at the site).
Best Time of Year:	Winter, for wildfowl.
Nearby Sites:	The woods and Southern riverbank of the Tyne at Wylam (one stop West of Blaydon, and with an hourly or better service) also hold wildfowl and waders (such as sandpipers), but are also noted for species such as dipper and sand martin, and for smaller birds attracted by the trees.
Notes:	

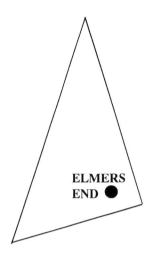

ELMERS
END ●

```
┌─────────────────────────────┐
│                             │
│  SOUTH NORWOOD              │
│  COUNTRY PARK               │
│                             │
└─────────────────────────────┘
```

County:	London.
Map:	Sheet 177 ref. TQ356684.
Nearest Stations:	Elmers End; Birkbeck.
Distance (m):	100-400 (depending on station).
Timetable no.:	204.
Rail Service:	**Elmers End**: Half-hourly service from Charing Cross via Waterloo, London Bridge, Lewisham and Catford Bridge to Hayes. Shuttle service (not Sundays) to Addiscombe (on the outskirts of Croydon).

Time taken: Catford Bridge 9 mins, Hayes 9 mins, Lewisham 13 mins, London Bridge 21 mins, Charing Cross 28 mins.

Peaks: Trains diverted at London Bridge to Cannon Street, with additional services to Charing Cross without calling at Lewisham.

Connections available at Catford for Peckham Rye; at Lewisham for Sidcup, Blackheath, Bexley and Dartford; at London Bridge for Greenwich and LUL's Northern line; at Waterloo for the Bakerloo line.

Birkbeck: Half-hourly service (not Sundays) from Victoria via Clapham Junc. (connections for Richmond, Wimbledon etc.), Balham (for Thornton Heath, LUL's Northern line)

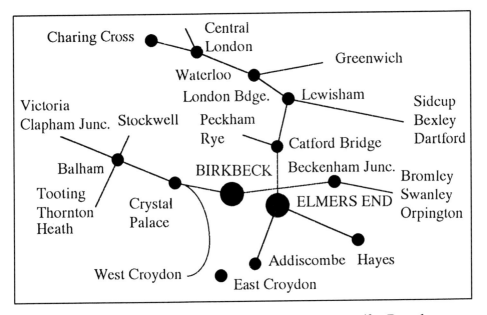

and Crystal Palace to Beckenham Junc. (for Bromley, Swanley and Orpington)).

Note: The proposed Croydon tram system will take over and extend the Addiscombe branch into Central Croydon (including East and West Croydon stations), will pass through the park, and run parallel to the existing BR service from Birkbeck to Beckenham Junction.

Local Facilities: Elmers End and Birkbeck both have the usual range of local shops; in both cases these are on the opposite side of the railway to the park.

Habitat: Disused sewage works, now mostly scrub but with a pond and a fringe of woodland.

Access: Turn left (North-West) outside Elmers End station; access is to the left. A series of footpaths lead around the reserve and to South Norwood.

Likely Sightings: Smaller birds such as linnet, buntings, finches, tits, warblers; gulls, ducks, heron; kestrel.

Best Time of Year: Avoid popular recreational times.

Notes:

THE SWALE

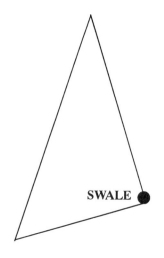

SWALE ●

County:	Kent.
Map:	Sheet 178 ref. TQ900700
Nearest Station:	Swale.
Distance (m):	100 .
Timetable no.:	213 .
Rail Service:	Hourly shuttle service between Sittingbourne and Sheerness-on-Sea.
	Time taken: 8 mins to both Sittingbourne and Sheerness. *Connections* available at Sittingbourne for Chatham, Bromley South, Faversham, Herne Bay, Canterbury East, Margate and Ramsgate.
Local Facilities:	Mobile caravan serving hot dogs etc. in lay-by on other side of road opposite station.
Habitat:	Marsh, estuary, meadow.
Access:	Opposite the station entrance through the small car park at the water's edge.
Likely Sightings:	Wagtails, warblers; marsh harrier, grebes; waders (including avocet); gulls. A 8km circular walk following the Saxon Shore Way around Chetney marshes gives views of the marshes from a causeway and also permits Funton Creek to be overlooked, which is likely to increase the

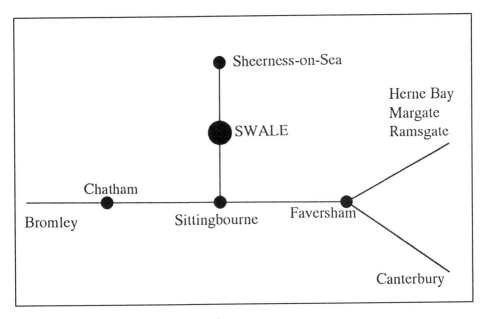

number of species seen.

Best Time of Year: Summer; the area is very exposed.

Notes:

The Grey Heron favour areas of shallow water with protective vegetation, and is therefore at home in marshy areas such as estuaries; it stands motionless before spearing fish. [J.H. Hume

TAMAR ESTUARY

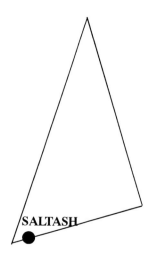

SALTASH

County: Cornwall/Devon.
Map: Sheet 201 ref. SX433593.
Nearest Station: Saltash.
Distance (m):   400.
Timetable no.:   135.
Rail Service: Irregular service (two-hourly off-peak, hourly in the peaks)
                   between Plymouth and Penzance via Liskeard and Truro.
                   Some services extended beyond Plymouth to Exeter and
                   Bristol.
                   Time taken: Plymouth 12 mins, Liskeard 18 mins, Truro 70
                   mins, Penzance 107 mins.
                   Sundays: Extremely limited service.
                   Connections available at Plymouth for Gunnislake, Totnes
                   and Exeter, at Liskeard for Looe, and at Truro for
                   Falmouth. Note that connections are also available between
                   Penzance services and the branch lines to Newquay and St
                   Ives at Par and St Erth respectively.
Local Facilities: Local shops and pub only.
Habitat: Estuarine mudflats.
Access: Keep on public roads following the Western shore, and
                   pass under the Tamar Bridge.
Likely Sightings: Gulls; waders (including avocet, sandpipers, godwits,

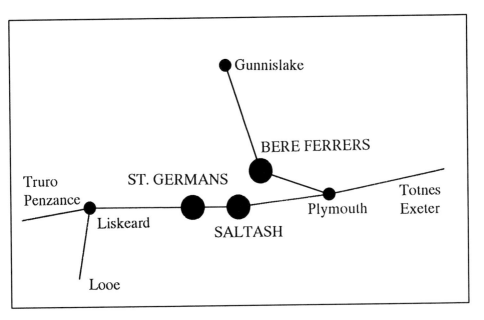

greenshank); terns.

Best Time of Year: Autumn (for passage migrants); Winter (for waders).

Nearby Sites: The upper reaches of the Lynher River can easily be viewed from St Germans Quay, only a 400 metre walk from the station, whilst Bere Ferrers provides good access (800-1000m) to both the Tamar and Tavy estuaries. St Germans is one stop (7 mins) West of Saltash with a similar train service; Bere Ferrers is on the Gunnislake branch (approx. two-hourly service from Plymouth (not Sundays September-mid May), journey time 20 mins).

Notes:

TYNE ESTUARY

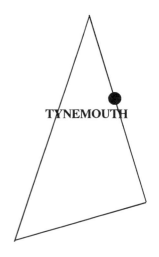

TYNEMOUTH

County:	Tyne and Wear.
Map:	Sheet 88 ref. NZ375690.
Nearest Station:	Tynemouth (T&W Metro).
Distance (m):	800.
Timetable no.:	n/a.
Rail Service:	Trains every 10-12 minutes around the Tyneside loop to/ from Newcastle via Benton or Wallsend. Trains via Benton continue through Newcastle to Gateshead and Pelaw (see map).

Time taken: Central Newcastle 25 mins (approx).
Connections available on the Metro at South Gosforth for the Newcastle Airport branch, and mainline services from Newcastle Central to Berwick, Edinburgh, Hexham, Carlisle, Durham, Darlington, Sunderland and Hartlepool.

Local Facilities:	Local shops, pubs etc.
Habitat:	Rocky coast and beaches; pier.
Access:	Past the ruined castle to Black Middens rocks and North Pier (the latter at discretion of Harbour Authority, but usually open).
Likely Sightings:	Gulls, terns; waders (at Black Middens); fulmar; cormorant; seaducks e.g. eider, velvet scoter (from North Pier).

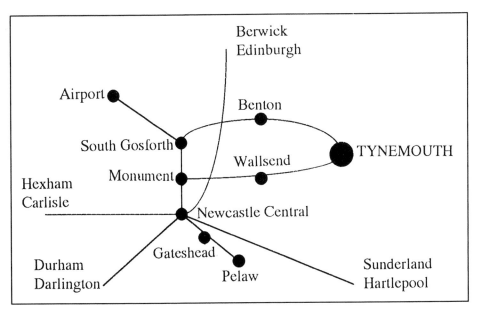

Best Time of Year: Autumn—possibility of migrating seabirds e.g. shearwaters, skuas.

Notes:

The Herring Gull is an aggressive bird which has adapted well to disturbance by people, as it will eat almost anything. Whilst it is common in docks (as seen here), it will also scavenge at rubbish tips. [N.G. Harris

TYWI ESTUARY

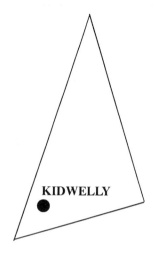

KIDWELLY

County:	Dyfed.
Map:	Sheet 159 ref. SN400064.
Nearest Station:	Kidwelly.
Distance (m):	200.
Timetable no.:	128.
Rail Service:	Broadly two-hourly service from Swansea via Llanelli to Pembroke Dock via Carmarthen and Tenby. Some services to Milford Haven also stop.
	Time taken: Llanelli 11 mins, Carmarthen 20 mins (approx), Swansea 30 mins, Tenby 68 mins, Pembroke Dock 1 hour 35 mins.
	Connections available at Carmarthen for Milford Haven; at Llanelli for Llandrindod Wells; and at Swansea for Neath, Bridgend and Cardiff.
Local Facilities:	Local shops, pubs etc.
Access:	Over the level crossing adjacent to the station.
Habitat:	Marshes, estuarine mudflats.
Likely Sightings:	Waders; gulls; wildfowl.
Best Time of Year:	Winter—increased concentrations of waders and ducks.
Nearby Sites:	The smaller village of Ferryside (one station, 7 mins) to the North has a similar train service and is nearer the main channel of the river.

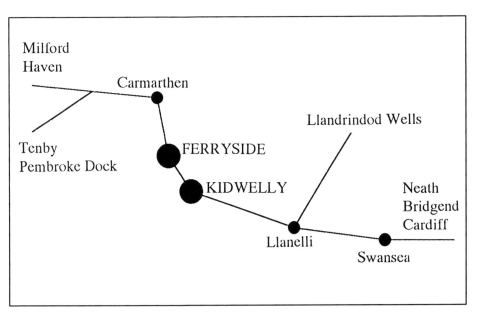

Milford
Haven

Carmarthen

Llandrindod Wells

Tenby
Pembroke Dock

FERRYSIDE

KIDWELLY

Neath
Bridgend
Cardiff

Llanelli

Swansea

Notes:

The Coot is a bird of ponds, rivers and shallow water, typically feeding on aquatic plants. [*N.G. Harris*

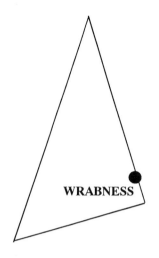

WRABNESS

County:	Essex.
Map:	Sheet 168 ref. TM185317.
Nearest Station:	Wrabness.
Distance (m):	500.
Timetable no.:	11.
Rail Service:	Hourly shuttle service between Manningtree and Harwich Town.
	Peaks: Some through services to Colchester and London Liverpool St.
	Time taken: Manningtree 10 mins, Harwich Town 12 mins, Colchester 18 mins, Liverpool Street 85 mins.
	Connections available at Manningtree for Ipswich, Colchester, Chelmsford and Liverpool Street.
Local Facilities:	Public house; hides overlooking Copperas Bay (an RSPB reserve).
Habitat:	Deciduous wood (Stour Wood); saltmarsh and mudflats.
Access:	Footpaths off the minor road bridge immediately to the East of the station.
Likely Sightings:	Nightingale, woodpeckers and warblers; Brent geese; waders including black-tailed godwit, grey plover, redshank, dunlin; ducks e.g. pintail and shelduck.
Best Time of Year:	Summer for the woods; Autumn/Winter for the mudflats.

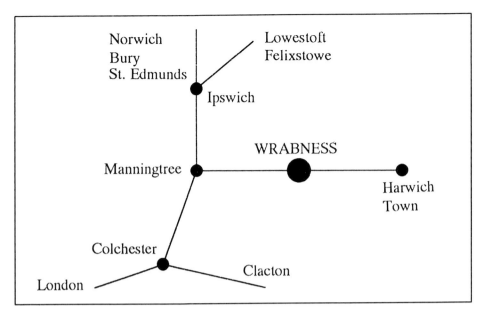

Norwich
Bury
St. Edmunds

Lowestoft
Felixstowe

Ipswich

WRABNESS

Manningtree

Harwich
Town

Colchester

Clacton

London

Notes:

The Canada Goose is not a native British bird, but is an aggressive bird which has colonised quickly and spread widely. So successful has it been, that it is now being culled in some areas to protect vegetation and indigenous bird species. [N.G. Harris

Important Information
FOR ALL BIRDWATCHERS

Each month Bird Watching
magazine covers just about
everything you need to
know ...
What birds have been seen in
your county; new places to go
bird watching; how to
improve your identification
skills; rare bird sightings; best
buys in binoculars;
conservation news and
stunning photography.
Pick up all you need to know
from your newsagent on the
30th of every month.

Index of Stations

Lyndhurst Road	85	Staines	81
Millom	75	Starcross	46
Montrose	82	Sugar Loaf Halt	31
Morfa Mawddach	18	Sunningdale	81
Neston	67	Swale	108
North Queensferry	73	Teignmouth	47
Northumberland Park	45	Thatcham	71
Penarth	90	Theale	70
Ponders End	45	The Lakes	34
Ravenglass	97	Thetford	29
Ribblehead	43	Thurgarton	21
Rye House	94	Tonfanau	19
St Bees	96	Tottenham Hale	45
St Germans	111	Troon	51
Saltash	110	Tynemouth	112
Sandy	100	Warblington	33
Scotscalder	57	West Kirby	66
Seaford	17	Weymouth	92
Severn Beach	102	Whatstandwell	88
Severn Tunnel Junction	103	Wrabness	116
Shoreham-by-Sea	14	Wylam	104
Silverdale	74		
Southbourne	33		
Southease	17		

Notes:

Notes:

Notes:

Notes:

Notes:

Notes:

Notes:

Notes: